W9-CDM-719

A Pro/Con Look at Homeland Security

Safety vs. Liberty After 9/11

A Pro/Con Look at Homeland Security

Safety vs. Liberty After 9/11

ISSUES IN FOCUS TODAY

Kathiann M. Kowalski

 Enslow Publishers, Inc.
40 Industrial Road
Box 398
Berkeley Heights, NJ 07922
USA
http://www.enslow.com

This book is dedicated to my daughter, Bethany Meissner.

Library of Congress Cataloging-in-Publication Data

Kowalski, Kathiann M., 1955-
  A pro/con look at homeland security : safety vs. liberty after 9/11 / Kathiann M. Kowalski.
      p. cm.— (Issues in focus today)
  Summary: "Examines Homeland Security in the United States after the tragedy of 9/11 and discusses the differences between keeping Americans safe and taking away their civil liberties"—Provided by publisher.
  Includes bibliographical references and index.
  ISBN-13: 978-0-7660-2914-9
  ISBN-10: 0-7660-2914-X
  1. Civil rights—United States—Juvenile literature. 2. National security—United States—Juvenile literature. 3. September 11 Terrorist Attacks, 2001—Juvenile literature. 4. War on Terrorism, 2001—Juvenile literature. 5. Terrorism—United States—Prevention—Juvenile literature. I. Title.
  JC599.U5K68 2008
  363.340973—dc22

                                        2007024524

Printed in the United States of America

10 9 8 7 6 5 4 3 2 1

To Our Readers: We have done our best to make sure all Internet addresses in this book were active and appropriate when we went to press. However, the author and the publisher have no control over and assume no liability for the material available on those Internet sites or on other Web sites they may link to. Any comments or suggestions can be sent by e-mail to comments@enslow.com or to the address on the back cover.

Illustration Credits: Clem Albers, pp. 24, 91; Jocelyn Augustino/FEMA News Photo, pp. 5, 76; Andrea Booher/FEMA News Photo, pp. 3, 5, 7, 78; Kathiann M. Kowalski, pp. 5, 36, 39, 43, 83, 87, 93, 95, 103; Courtesy of Massachusetts Bay Transportation Authority, p. 68; National Archives and Records Administration, pp. 17, 20, 89; National Security Agency, p. 14; Gerald L. Nino/U.S. Customs and Border Protection, pp. 5, 32, 46, 53, 60, 64, 72, 97, 99; Courtesy of Cpt. Jaime Parker, U.S. Army, Chemical Corps, pp. 5, 22; Michael Rieger/FEMA News Photo, pp. 5, 10; James R. Tourtellote/U.S. Customs and Border Protection, pp. 49, 57; U.S. Customs and Border Protection, pp. 81, 101; U.S. Department of Homeland Security, p. 82; U.S. Senate Historical Office, p. 26.

Cover Illustration: Gerald L. Nino/U.S. Customs and Border Protection (large photo); BananaStock (inset photo).

Contents

On September 11, 2001, terrorists hijacked four airliners. Two jets crashed into the World Trade Center in New York. One hit the Pentagon near Washington, D.C. The fourth crashed in Pennsylvania.

The September 11 attacks killed 2,819 people.[1] They also changed life for millions of Americans. Homeland security became a top national priority.

America Under Attack

Early on September 11, 2001, two planes took off for Los Angeles from Boston's Logan International Airport. Each Boeing 767 jet carried about ten thousand gallons of jet fuel.

On American Airlines Flight 11, hijackers killed three people. Then they stormed into the cockpit and took over the plane. Suddenly, the jet made a sharp turn toward New York City.

Two flight attendants, Madeline "Amy" Sweeney and Betty Ong, alerted American Airlines with cell phones. Suddenly, the aircraft lost altitude.

"We are flying low," Sweeney said. "Oh my God, we are way too low."

At 8:46 A.M., the plane crashed into the north tower of New York's 110-story World Trade Center. Within two minutes, CNN news reported the crash. As smoke billowed from the burning skyscraper, fire department crews rushed in.

Meanwhile, other terrorists had seized United Airlines Flight 175. At 9:03 A.M., it slammed into the World Trade Center's south tower. Thousands of Americans saw the crash live on television.

People streamed down the skyscrapers' stairwells. Thousands found their way out. Others became hopelessly trapped, including everyone on the highest floors.

Some people jumped to their deaths rather than be burned alive. Others called family members on cell phones. "Please tell the children I love them," Frederick Varacchi told his sister from the north tower's 105th floor.[2]

At 9:59 A.M., the south tower of the World Trade Center collapsed. The north tower fell twenty-nine minutes later.

Meanwhile, five other terrorists had hijacked American Airlines Flight 77. The plane left Washington's Dulles International Airport at 8:20 A.M. At 9:37 A.M., it crashed into the Pentagon. The huge office building in Arlington, Virginia, is headquarters for America's Department of Defense. All on board the flight died, along with 125 people at the Pentagon.

One minute later, United Airlines Flight 93 swerved off

its route from Newark, New Jersey, to San Francisco. After a hairpin turn, the jet headed toward Washington, D.C.

Flight 93 passengers called family members on cell phones. They learned about the other attacks. Clearly, the hijackers planned to use their plane as a bomb too.

"If they're going to run this into the ground, we have to do something," Tom Burnett told his wife in California.[3] Together, passengers began ramming on the cockpit door. At 10:03 A.M., the plane crashed in rural Somerset County, Pennsylvania.[4]

At 11:45 A.M., President George W. Bush addressed the nation. "Freedom itself was attacked this morning by a faceless coward," he said. "And freedom will be defended."[5] America's war on terror had begun.

What Happened?

Within days, American intelligence agents intercepted a message. "We've hit the targets," it said. The message came from people linked to al-Qaeda, a terrorist network headed by Osama bin Laden.[6]

Definitions of terrorism vary. Justice Department rules say: "Terrorism includes the unlawful use of force and violence against persons or property to intimidate or coerce a government, the civilian population, or any segment thereof, in furtherance of political or social objectives."[7] The State Department defines terrorism as "premeditated, politically motivated violence perpetrated against noncombatant targets by subnational groups or clandestine agents, usually intended to influence an audience."[8] The Department of Defense uses yet another definition: "The calculated use of unlawful violence or threat of unlawful violence to inculcate fear; intended to coerce or to intimidate governments or societies in the pursuit of goals that are generally political, religious, or ideological."[9]

The terms used affect the scope of agencies' activities. Yet the different definitions share some common features.

In general, then, terrorism is the use or threat of unlawful violence to exert power over people through fear, for political, religious, or similar goals.

Terrorists do not just attack governments and their leaders. They also strike out at ordinary civilians. Publicity about the attacks multiplies the fear factor. Al-Qaeda is one of many terrorist groups in the twentieth and twenty-first centuries.

Workers begin the monumental job of cleaning up after the collapse of the World Trade Center. The terrorist attack left America, and the world, stunned.

Years before the September 11 attacks, Osama bin Laden had declared a *jihad*, or holy war, against the United States. He claimed that America's military presence in the Middle East was an act of aggression against the Muslim world. (Mecca in Saudi Arabia is Islam's holiest city.)

Most Muslims reject bin Laden's radical version of Islam. Still, he attracted many followers. After studying passenger lists, the government identified nineteen men who carried out the September 11 attacks. All had ties to al-Qaeda.

Oddly enough, airport security systems had flagged six of the men for more scrutiny. Despite that, all six boarded their planes. They carried knives and box cutters as weapons.

Also, some of the men were in the United States on expired visas. A visa allows someone from one nation to enter another country.

Several hijackers had gone to American flight schools too. Three took lessons in Florida. One went to schools in Arizona.

A fifth al-Qaeda member went to a Minnesota flight school. His instructor became suspicious and reported him. As a result, the government arrested Zacarias Moussaoui on immigration charges in August 2001. He later stood trial for conspiracy in the September 11 attacks.

Airport security rules have become much stricter since 2001. The government has also added programs to track foreigners, tighten borders, and trace possible terrorist activities.

Meanwhile, people wondered if the government might have prevented the September 11 attacks. In July, an e-mail had warned FBI

In general, terrorism is the use or threat of unlawful violence to exert power over people through fear, for political, religious, or similar goals.

headquarters that Osama bin Laden might be sending students to American flight schools. "These individuals will be in a position in the future to conduct terror activity against civil aviation targets," wrote Kenneth Williams at the Phoenix office.[10]

The FBI's Minneapolis office also raised questions about Moussaoui. Foreign intelligence agencies in Germany, Egypt, Jordan, and Russia claimed they passed along warnings about possible air attacks too.

Politicians, journalists, and other critics argued about whether to blame the Bush administration. Some wondered if former President Bill Clinton could have done more during his eight years of leadership. To address these concerns, Congress and the President set up the 9/11 Commission. The commission included five Republicans and five Democrats, plus more than six dozen staff members. The commission's report in 2004 reflected reviews of more than 2.5 million pages of documents, talks with more than 1,200 individuals, and public testimony from 160 witnesses.[11]

The 9/11 Commission found that clearly mistakes were made. Some were human errors, like failing to find weapons after two men set off metal detectors. Other failures resulted from inadequate procedures. For example, airports let several hijackers board planes even though they were on watch lists.

Likewise, the government lacked effective plans for responding to the attacks. Even before the commission's report came out, though, the government began a major overhaul of its security system.

Never Again!

"The only way to defeat terrorism as a threat to our way of life is to stop it, eliminate it, and destroy it where it grows," President Bush announced on September 20, 2001.[12] The United States had been at war before. However, its former enemies had been foreign countries and their agents.

Al-Qaeda and other terrorist groups act outside of governments. Countries have fixed locations. Terrorist groups do not.

Based on information that Osama bin Laden was in Afghanistan, American troops went there in October 2001.

They quickly unseated the ruling Taliban government, which had been helping al-Qaeda. They did not find bin Laden, however.

In March 2003, American troops went to Iraq. The U.S. government claimed that Saddam Hussein's government had links to al-Qaeda. It also said Iraq had weapons of mass destruction. Hussein's government fell, and President Bush appeared under a huge "Mission Accomplished" banner in May 2003.

More than four years later, though, evidence of the government's claims had not turned up. At the same time, fighting and attacks were still going on.

Meanwhile, the United States made significant changes to its antiterrorism programs at home. To start, President Bush created the Office of Homeland Security within the White House.

Congress also took action. On October 26, by a vote of 357 to 66, the House passed the USA PATRIOT Act of 2001. (The name stood for Uniting and Strengthening America by Providing Appropriate Tools Required to Intercept and Obstruct Terrorism; later it was known simply as the Patriot Act.) The Senate passed the act by a vote of 98 to 1.

Among other things, the Patriot Act expanded the government's ability to get documents and conduct searches dealing with suspected terrorism. In many cases, the government could do this without having to get a warrant signed by a judge. Civil liberties groups strongly oppose parts of the law. Nevertheless, Congress reauthorized and expanded the Patriot Act in 2006.

The Homeland Security Act of 2002 created the Department of Homeland Security (DHS). Led by former Pennsylvania governor Tom Ridge, DHS brought together the work of twenty-two federal agencies. The head of DHS has a cabinet-level job.

With about 208,000 employees as of 2007, DHS has become the third largest government agency.[13] It includes the

Transportation Security Administration (TSA), the Secret Service, the Coast Guard, and U.S. Customs and Border Protection. Its agencies also handle citizenship and immigration matters. The Federal Emergency Management Agency (FEMA) is within DHS too.

Outside of DHS, other agencies also track possible terrorist activity. They include the Federal Bureau of Investigation (FBI), the Central Intelligence Agency (CIA), the Defense Intelligence Agency, the National Counterterrorism Center, and the National Security Agency (NSA).

The National Security Agency is one of the government groups that tracks possible terrorist activity, along with the FBI, the CIA, and other agencies.

Congress has passed other laws too. A 2006 law gave federal agencies more leeway in interrogating suspected terrorists and convicting them of crimes. New laws may expand or shrink the government's powers.

Americans today feel the impact of stepped-up surveillance and government watchfulness. News reports include regular updates on the war on terror, both at home and abroad. Travelers especially face greater security hurdles at airports or border crossings.

Other homeland security activities are less obvious. Intelligence agencies review library records, financial data, and other information. They have conducted physical searches and listened in on international phone calls.

The government has also gathered call records for thousands of Americans. Plus, it has asked Internet providers to keep records for possible review.

The stepped-up security measures reassure some people, but they worry others. One question is whether the United States is doing enough to guard against terrorism. Critics like Clark Kent Ervin say terrorists could still exploit huge gaps in America's security systems. As a former inspector general of the Department of Homeland Security, Ervin's job was to investigate problems within the agency.[14]

Other critics say the United States is going overboard. They worry that the government wastes resources and oversteps the bounds of common sense.

More importantly, some critics claim, homeland security programs hamper Americans' rights under the Constitution. The American Civil Liberties Union (ACLU) and Electronic Frontier Foundation are leading critics in this camp.

Since 2001, homeland security has become a constant concern. The issue assumes even more significance in election years. Eager to win or keep their elected positions, politicians appeal to people's passions—and to their fears.

Some voters want a candidate who will be stronger on national security. Others want to be sure the government will preserve everyone's freedoms. Psychologists suggest that the choice depends on each voter's values and view of the world. As you read, consider how your values affect your position on homeland security.

Since its beginning, the United States has faced threats both at home and abroad. The twenty-first century's focus on terrorism differs in significant ways. Yet there are similarities to the past.

A Young Nation

France helped the United States win the Revolutionary War. Then a revolution toppled its government in 1789. Afterward, France seized American ships that traded with its old enemy, Great Britain. In America's view, this was piracy.

The resulting "Quasi-War" with France lasted from 1798

until 1800. Congress rescinded America's prior treaties with France in 1798. It also passed the Alien and Sedition Acts.

The Alien and Sedition Acts made it a crime to write, speak, or publish anything "false, scandalous and malicious" against the government. It was also a crime to "excite" against the government "the hatred of the good people of the United States."[1]

Lawmakers hoped to head off any revolution in the United States. However, President John Adams's administration used the laws against political foes. Republican editors, publishers, and even a congressman faced charges.

Republicans became outraged. In 1798, the Kentucky and Virginia Resolutions asserted the states' right to reject laws like the Alien and Sedition Acts. After all, the First Amendment guaranteed freedom of speech and of the press. Laws saying otherwise went beyond the federal government's power.

In 1800, anger over the federal laws helped Thomas Jefferson and other Republicans win elections. The Sedition Act expired by 1802. However, versions of the Alien Act remained law until the twentieth century.

A Nation Torn Apart

During the War of 1812 America battled Great Britain. Afterward, the country's independence seemed secure. The United States was far away from most of the powerful countries. Foreign attacks seemed unlikely.

Except for the Mexican-American War (1846–1848), the United States enjoyed several decades of peace. At home, though, tensions mounted between the North and the South.

In 1861, the Civil War broke out. President Abraham Lincoln worried about riots and potential uprisings. He suspended the writ of habeas corpus in 1861.

The writ of habeas corpus says the government must bring a prisoner into court for a ruling on the lawfulness of the imprisonment. Maryland cavalry officer John Merryman challenged Lincoln's action after the army arrested him.

In those days, Supreme Court justices took turns as federal circuit court judges. Merryman's case came before Supreme Court Justice Roger Taney in *Ex parte Merryman.* (*Ex parte* means that technically only one side was before the court.)

Taney ruled that the president could not suspend the writ of habeas corpus. Only Congress had that power under the Constitution. Also, the military's power extended only to people subject to the rules of war.

Otherwise, civil authorities were in charge. If the military could just seize power "at its discretion," Taney wrote, "the people of the United States are no longer living under a government of laws."[2]

Lincoln ignored the court order. Eventually Merryman got out on bail. Meanwhile, the government held hundreds of people without benefit of habeas corpus. Prisoners included mayors, newspaper editors, and members of the Maryland legislature. Congress finally approved the president's actions with the Habeas Corpus Act of 1863.

Lincoln also argued that the government could try citizens for various crimes in special military tribunals. The Supreme Court rejected that argument in *Ex parte Milligan.* By the time it ruled in 1866, the war was over. Nonetheless, the Court felt the principles were important.

As long as citizen courts stay open, Justice David Davis wrote, the right to trial in a regular judicial court is "one of the plainest constitutional provisions." Davis added:

"It could be well said that a country, preserved at the sacrifice of all the cardinal principles of liberty, is not worth the cost of preservation. Happily, it is not so."[3]

Similar issues would arise again during the twenty-first century's war on terror.

All major battles in World War I (1914–1919) took place on

Abraham Lincoln suspended the writ of habeas corpus in 1861, following the outbreak of the Civil War, and ignored the court order that found this unlawful.

foreign soil or at sea. Nevertheless, many people at home opposed the war effort. In *Schenck* v. *United States*, the Supreme Court upheld the conviction of a man who printed leaflets in favor of resisting the draft. Justice Oliver Wendell Holmes wrote:

> The question in every case is whether the words used are used in such circumstances and are of such a nature as to create a clear and present danger that they will bring about the substantive evils that Congress has a right to prevent.... When a nation is at war many things which might be said in time of peace are such a hindrance to its efforts that their utterance will not be endured so long as men fight.[4]

The Supreme Court also upheld a conviction of socialist politician Eugene Debs after he praised draft resisters. Schenck and Debs might not get convictions today. Yet government supporters still worry whether public criticism will hinder homeland security efforts.

World War II—America Under Attack

On Sunday, December 7, 1941, Japanese planes attacked America's Pacific Fleet at Pearl Harbor in Hawaii. The strike killed 2,388 Americans and injured more than 1,000 others. Twenty American ships and more than 300 aircraft were damaged or destroyed.

Before the attack, tensions had been building between Japan and the United States. Meanwhile, war had broken out in Europe. Nazi Germany had invaded Czechoslovakia, Poland, and other countries.

Now the United States could no longer sit on the sidelines. On December 8, 1941, Congress declared war on Japan. Three days later, Nazi Germany and Fascist Italy declared war on America too.

Most of World War II's battles would again be fought abroad. Americans at home were afraid, though. Japan's surprise attack succeeded because "fifth column" spies passed along information about the U.S. Navy and its ships.[5] A "fifth column" group seems to be ordinary people. But it supports a country's enemies by undermining it from within.

Americans worried that a "fifth column" was at work outside Hawaii too. For decades, the number of Japanese Americans had risen in western states. Many people worried about their loyalty.

In response, President Roosevelt issued Executive Order 9066. "The successful prosecution of the war requires every possible protection against espionage and against sabotage,"

On December 7, 1941, Japanese planes attacked the U.S. Pacific Fleet at Pearl Harbor, Hawaii, leading to America's entry into World War II.

it said. Under the order, Secretary of War Henry Stinson designated "military areas."[6] The government could limit people's right to stay in or enter those areas.

In some places, the military ordered Japanese Americans to stay home every night. In other areas—mostly in California, Washington, Arizona, and Oregon—Japanese Americans had to leave their homes entirely.

Longtime citizenship or residence made no difference. No suspicion of actual wrongdoing was necessary, either. The government herded nearly one hundred twenty thousand Japanese Americans onto trains and took them to ten "relocation centers."

Evacuees could take very little with them. And they had no time to sell homes or other property for fair value. People lost homes, jobs, and businesses.

Just like prisoner-of-war camps, relocation centers had bleak barracks with group bathrooms. Manned guard towers and barbed-wire fences kept people inside.

Fred Korematsu defied a relocation order. In 1944, the Supreme Court upheld his criminal conviction. In the majority opinion, Justice Hugo Black wrote:

> We cannot say that the war-making branches of the Government did not have ground for believing that in a critical hour such persons could not readily be isolated and separately dealt with, and constituted a menace to the national defense and safety, which demanded that prompt and adequate measures be taken to guard against it.[7]

Justices Robert Jackson, Frank Murphy, and Owen Roberts dissented. America was also fighting Germany and Italy. Yet German Americans and Italian Americans did not have to move. In Justice Murphy's view, forced relocation of Japanese Americans went "over 'the very brink of constitutional power.'" It fell "into the ugly abyss of racism."[8]

Years afterward, most Americans realized that the government had acted wrongly. The Civil Liberties Act of 1988 formally admitted that the government had violated Japanese Americans' "basic civil liberties and constitutional rights."[9] The apology could not undo the past, though.

Indeed, if the government could take such drastic action one time, how far might it go in the future? Would the Supreme

Japanese Americans wait to board the train that will take them to an internment camp. President Franklin Roosevelt issued an order that deprived them of their civil liberties out of concern over security during World War II.

Court again defer so broadly to the executive branch? These questions resurface during the war on terror.

Spy Agencies and the Cold War

After World War II, the United States faced a new threat: the Cold War. From the 1950s through the 1980s, the United States and its allies worried about the spread of communism. The Soviet Union and other Communist countries took over private businesses. They also restricted rights like freedom of speech and religion.

Both sides had nuclear weapons, and all-out war was a real risk. In the field abroad, the CIA spied on military and political enemies. At home, the government investigated people who might promote communism.

During the early 1950s, Senator Joseph McCarthy (R-Wis.) led the hunt. His Senate committee called hundreds of people to testify. State governments also started loyalty boards, or panels, to investigate their employees.

One goal was to keep Communists from undermining America and its policies. Yet the flimsiest "evidence" could brand someone as a Communist. Many people became "black-listed," or unable to get work. Anti-Communist fervor destroyed many careers.

In 1952, for example, the Supreme Court upheld a New York law saying no one could teach in public schools if the state believed the person was a Communist or otherwise subversive. Such people could speak and meet on their own. But they had no right to a government job.

In dissent, Justice William O. Douglas argued that the law imposed "guilt by association." It even encouraged citizens to spy on one another. "What happens under this law is typical of what happens in a police state," Douglas objected.[10]

McCarthyism began to wane after CBS reporter Edward R. Murrow aired a controversial "Report on Joseph R. McCarthy"

During the 1950s, Senator Joseph McCarthy led a hunt to rid the United States of Communists, destroying the lives of many on scant evidence. Today, the term "McCarthyism" refers to efforts to discredit people by challenging their patriotism on flimsy grounds.

in March 1954. The ABC network also aired some of McCarthy's hearings live. Americans saw the panel's bullying and badgering. By the end of the year, the Senate itself censured McCarthy for his conduct. (To censure something is to formally disapprove of it.)

McCarthyism is now a negative term. It means trying to discredit people with flimsy claims of disloyalty. Questions about patriotism would arise again in the debate over homeland security.

Worldwide Threats

Starting in 1961, Americans faced a new security challenge: aircraft hijacking. After Fidel Castro took over Cuba in 1959, the United States broke off diplomatic ties with that country. Many people fled from Cuba. Others, like Antuilo Ramierez Ortiz, wanted to go there. In 1961, Ortiz forced a National Airlines plane to land in Havana, and Cuba let him stay. More hijackings followed.

Some airliners began having armed guards. Yet hijackings rose from 1968 to 1972. By the 1970s, most airports had metal detectors for finding weapons.

New threats arose worldwide during the 1970s. Palestinian terrorists attacked passengers on El Al, the Israeli airline, at the Munich Airport in 1970. Two years later, other Palestinian terrorists kidnapped eleven Israeli athletes at the Munich Olympics. Also in 1972, Irish Republican Army terrorists killed over a dozen people in Northern Ireland.

In 1973, an unknown terrorist group attacked at the Rome Airport, destroying a plane and killing more than two dozen people. In Italy, the Red Brigades' crimes included kidnapping president-to-be Aldo Moro in 1978. The Baader-Meinhoff gang opposed West Germany's government and killed more than thirty people during the 1970s.

American diplomats also became targets. A group called

Black September murdered Ambassador Cleo Noel and other diplomats in Sudan in 1973. Snipers shot Ambassador Rodger Davies during a 1974 demonstration in Cyprus. Unknown assassins killed Ambassador Francis Meloy, Jr., and counselor Robert Waring in Lebanon in 1976.

Attacks occurred within the United States too. In 1975, a Puerto Rican group set off a bomb in Manhattan. It killed four people and injured five dozen others. That same year, the Weather Underground group caused an explosion at a Department of State bathroom in Washington, D.C.

As these examples show, terrorists act independently of countries' governments. Attacks stun people with their boldness and cruelty. A terrorist group can have many members linked together in a network or organization. Or it can be just a few people with similar views.

A terrorist group can have many members linked together in a network or organization, or it can be just a few people with similar views.

Terrorist attacks are certainly crimes. As a general rule, the police could arrest anyone who committed kidnapping, murder, assault, battery, or intentional destruction of property. But just as terrorism differs from conventional war, it also differs from ordinary crime.

Terrorists generally have a political, religious, or other agenda. They crave publicity. Terrorists often plan and carry out crimes on a grander scale than other criminals. They want to instill fear in people.

Terrorism was not a major issue in the 1970s, but it was a growing concern. Meanwhile, some people wondered if America's intelligence agencies went too far in their work. A Senate committee led by Senator Frank Church (D-Idaho) began hearings in 1975. For two years, the committee reviewed claims of abuses by the CIA, the FBI, and others. Those hearings raised real concerns about citizens' rights and liberties.

In response, Congress passed the Foreign Intelligence Surveillance Act (FISA). The 1978 law affirmed the government's broad power to guard against foreign threats. However, the law set out rules.

If the government believed someone was an agent of a foreign government, it would not need to go to a regular court before doing electronic surveillance. However, the agency would need a warrant from a special panel of judges under FISA. The agency did not need probable cause to suspect criminal activity. But it would need some link to a foreign government or its agents.

In an emergency, the government could eavesdrop on phone calls first and get the FISA warrant later. Starting in the 1990s, FISA warrants allowed searches of physical property too. Under FISA, the government did not give notice of activities. No one wanted to tip off the targets of an investigation.

By that time, terrorists made dozens of other attacks. In 1983, the Islamic Jihad group bombed the American embassy in Lebanon. That same year, suicide truck bombers attacked American and French barracks in Lebanon.

In 1985, Lebanese Hezbollah terrorists hijacked a TWA flight in Europe and killed an American hostage. A Palestinian group blew up a TWA flight in 1986. In 1988, Libyan terrorists blew up a Pan Am flight over Scotland and killed 259 people.

Terrorism continued during the 1990s. In 1993, a bomb at the World Trade Center garage killed six people and injured about one thousand others. In 1998, bombs exploded at American embassies in Kenya and Tanzania. And in 2000, terrorists attacked the U.S.S. *Cole*, a navy warship, in Yemen.

The United States believes al-Qaeda caused these attacks. After the embassy attacks in 1998, President Bill Clinton ordered bombings of al-Qaeda training camps. However, the bombings did not get bin Laden or his top leaders.

"We did what we thought we could," President Clinton said in 2001. Meanwhile, he said, the government stopped several planned attacks. They included plots to blow up planes flying from Los Angeles and plans to kill Pope John Paul II.[11]

Foreigners were not the only terrorists. Starting in 1978, mail bombs killed or maimed more than two dozen people. Authorities finally arrested the "Unabomber," Theodore Kaczynski, in 1996.

Americans also destroyed the Albert P. Murrah federal building in Oklahoma City in 1995. Until 2001, the bombing was the largest terrorist attack within America's borders. Timothy McVeigh was executed for the crime. His coconspirator, Terry Nichols, was sentenced to life in prison.

Since September 11

The September 11 attacks stunned Americans. Thousands of people died sudden, violent deaths. Plus, the terrorists' bold planning was frightening. Americans felt vulnerable.

Bioterrorism—attacks that cause disease—became another fear. In late 2001, an unknown person or group sent anthrax bacteria to dozens of people. Targets included two U.S. senators and members of the media. Twenty-two people became ill. Five of them died.

Since 2001, the American public has had constant reminders about the war on terror. Reports about wars in Iraq, Afghanistan, and the Middle East fuel debates about threats from abroad.

At home, Americans face heightened security. Airline travelers face strict limits and lines for screening. Government buildings and large public facilities have stricter security too. Bag checks and frisking have become common even at events such as professional football games and concerts.

Homeland security makes the headlines too. In August 2006, for example, Americans learned about a plot to blow up planes with materials disguised as ordinary drinks or other liquids. British police arrested two dozen suspects involved in the plot.

Other times, the news is about efforts to track possible terrorists. Few people question the need to prevent future attacks. However, some of the government's actions raise significant questions.

The scope of the government's scrutiny is one issue. The government says it targets terrorists. However, some people worry that those efforts will curb Americans' basic rights.

The next chapter explores criticisms that civil rights groups have raised about homeland security. Chapter 4 will then look at arguments from the government's supporters.

Don't Sacrifice Civil Liberties!

Since 2001, homeland security has become a major priority. The government has questioned thousands of people. It has built a huge database with over 659 million records. It has searched through financial data, communications, and other sources.

Critics say some measures go too far. They fear the United States is sacrificing civil liberties in the name of fighting terrorism. In their view, that is too much to pay for the illusion of safety.

Enemies of the State

People who commit terrorist acts or help their networks draw little sympathy. Yet no one deserves to be tortured or abused, say civil rights groups.

Some people caught in Afghanistan and Iraq were handcuffed and left without food or water for more than a day. Others endured tortures like water-boarding—being strapped on a board and dunked as if drowning. Prisoners suffered crude humiliation too.

The CIA has also made various "extraordinary renditions"— kidnapping and delivery of prisoners to other countries for interrogation and imprisonment. In one case, Italian prosecutors said, CIA agents kidnapped a man from Milan. He endured torture and spent four years in an Egyptian prison.[1] In another case, a German citizen was grabbed while vacationing in Macedonia. He said he spent months in a secret CIA prison in Afghanistan.[2]

Such treatment violates basic human rights. Also, critics say, torture does not yield trustworthy information. People will say anything to stop the pain. Also, if the government tortures some suspects, what will stop it from doing the same to others?

Torture reports tarnish America's reputation. Whether accurate or not, Senator Jay Rockefeller (D-W.Va.) says that they have "hindered counterterrorism efforts with our allies."[3] Also, other countries might treat American prisoners badly in return.

Beyond that, the United States has held hundreds of people for months and even years without specific charges. When it did bring charges, the government wanted to use military commissions instead of regular courts. Military commissions have fewer protections for prisoners than regular courts do.

In 2006, the Supreme Court held that a military commission could not try Salim Ahmed Hamdan, a man captured in Afghanistan. The military commission did not have authority to deal with the general conspiracy charge. Also, the Geneva Conventions protected him and other prisoners. Those treaties set out the rights of prisoners of war.

That did not end the issue. Under the Constitution, Congress defines the federal courts' jurisdiction. Lawmakers who supported President Bush passed the Military Commissions Act of 2006. The law shifts prisoners' cases to military panels. It denies them any right of habeas corpus. It also relaxes rules about evidence that can be used in their trials.

The law also deals with how the government can treat people it believes are enemy combatants. It forbids grave breaches of the Geneva Conventions, such as rape, torture, and cruel and inhuman treatment like water-boarding. However, the executive branch's judgment might allow other extreme interrogation methods.

"It is a sad day when the rubber-stamp Congress undercuts our freedoms, assaults our Constitution and lets the terrorists achieve something they could never win on the battlefield," said Senator Patrick Leahy, (D-Vt.).[4] "Nothing could be further from the American values we all hold in our hearts than the Military Commissions Act," noted ACLU executive director Anthony Romero.[5]

In April 2007, the Supreme Court declined to decide whether the Military Commissions Act is constitutional. However, several justices warned that they might review the issue in the future.[6]

Meanwhile, the 2006 elections had changed the makeup of Congress. In 2007, Congress started looking at bills to change or repeal the Military Commissions Act. Senator Christopher Dodd (D-Conn.) sponsored one bill. He agreed that national security is important. "But," he added, "those who ask us to choose between national security and moral authority are offering us a false choice, and a dangerous one."[7]

The "Usual Suspects"

Homeland security investigations focused on people inside the United States too. After the September 11 attacks, the Justice Department rounded up hundreds of Muslim Arabs living in the United States. Many had broken immigration laws. However, few had any provable links to terrorism.

Nonetheless, a 2003 report by the Justice Department's inspector general found that hundreds of those people endured physical and verbal abuse. Many were kept in cramped, brightly lit cells for over twenty-three hours each day. They often could not communicate with families or lawyers, either.[8]

Arab-American organizations and civil rights groups objected. In their view, the massive arrests were based solely on people's race and religion. That went against the Constitution's guarantee of equal protection under the law.

In addition, the government's harsh treatment seemed to ignore basic rights. The Fifth Amendment says persons cannot be deprived of liberty or property unless the government follows rules known as "due process of law." The Sixth Amendment says accused persons have the right to know the charges against them, the right to a speedy trial, and the right to counsel. The Eighth Amendment forbids cruel and unusual punishment.

The Center for Constitutional Rights sued on behalf of people who had been held in Brooklyn, New York. In 2006, a federal court dismissed charges based on racial profiling. However, the judge let them sue on claims of mistreatment and religious discrimination. The case was pending as this book went to press.

More controversy arose over the Justice Department's "Interview Project." The government questioned more than five thousand people of Arab and Muslim background. It claimed the interviews were voluntary. However, many people feared reprisals if they did not answer questions. People also complained about discrimination afterward.

"First, it is wrong to single out innocent people based on their ethnicity or religion," argued James Zogby, president of the Arab American Institute. "This runs contrary to the uniquely American ideal of equal protection under the law." The government's "wide net" also wasted law enforcement resources and alienated many people.[10]

Many people became alarmed when reports detailed the extent of government surveillance programs.

Routine searches raise problems too. Everyone goes through searches or questioning at airports, border crossings, and various public facilities. However, civil rights groups argue that some people get extra scrutiny because of race or ethnicity. They say that is both wrong and illegal.

In 2005, several Muslim Americans sued DHS after a lengthy delay at the U.S.–Canadian border. The group had been returning from a religious conference in Toronto. They felt they were held up just because of their ethnicity and religion. However, the trial court judge ruled in favor of DHS.

Appeals and other cases will likely raise the issue again. Meanwhile, some Muslim Americans feel uneasy about traveling. They worry about excessive DHS scrutiny.

At airports, the TSA handles security matters. To avoid claims about racial profiling, it sometimes has made random searches of passengers. That raised other problems, though. People felt that they were being hassled and harassed for no reason.

In response, the government has proposed "psychological profiling." Basically, agents would pick people for extra scrutiny based on their behavior. Agents would thus use their judgment. Yet civil rights groups worry that this method may be just another name for racial profiling.[11]

Stop Spying on Us!

Before 2001, information obtained under FISA could only be used for America's foreign intelligence work. Now the government can use information in criminal cases too. The Justice Department argued that the Patriot Act gave it this authority. The FISA judges agreed.

Civil rights groups saw this as a trick to get around the Fourth Amendment, which generally requires search warrants based on probable cause. Also, the FISA judges did not publish their opinions. Thus, no one would know the standards by which they let the government conduct secret searches. The Supreme Court did not review the case.

More furor erupted when news broke that the government did not always obey even FISA's more relaxed requirements. In 2005, *The New York Times* revealed that President Bush had let the NSA monitor international telephone calls and e-mails of "hundreds, perhaps thousands" of people within the United States without FISA warrants. Before 2002, the NSA had monitored only communications outside the United States. Current and former NSA workers told the newspaper about the program because they doubted its legality.[12]

> **Furor erupted when news broke that the government did not always obey even FISA's relaxed requirements.**

The government said its surveillance included only communications where at least one party was outside the country. Then *USA Today* revealed that the NSA had phone records for tens of millions of Americans. Large phone companies had turned over the records without their customers' permission.[13]

"'Trust us' isn't good enough," argued *USA Today*'s editors.[14] Phone companies have a legal duty to protect customers' privacy. When the government asked for records without warrants, it encouraged companies to break the law.

The agency denied listening in on ordinary Americans. Nonetheless, people felt outraged. In their view, the government had no right to private information.

"Most of us don't mind spying on al-Qaeda," noted Democratic National Committee chair Howard Dean. "We'd just like to not have them spy on my grandmother when I call her up six times."[15]

More concern arose when the Justice Department asked major Internet providers to keep data on customers' activities for two years, versus just a few weeks. The government could

People became accustomed to new airport security precautions after September 11. However, civil rights groups say that some people are singled out for special attention because of their race or ethnicity.

then seek that information for terrorism, pornography, or other law enforcement cases.

"I think that the request raises some really, really major privacy problems," said Lee Tien of the Electronic Frontier Foundation. It was like asking Internet providers to "become an arm of the government."[16]

The government's failure to disclose the full extent of its surveillance fed fears about the invasion of privacy. Some reports suggested that the NSA had secret rooms built at or near telecommunication company headquarters. That implied an ability to eavesdrop not only on phone calls, but also on data going through the Internet.

The government bought information from commercial databases as well. Among other things, agencies tried to spot possible identity or immigration fraud and to predict potential weapons smuggling.

Some critics questioned whether massive data mining was a worthwhile use of government time and money. Meanwhile, Jim Dempsey at the Center for Democracy and Technology worried about "the chilling effect that comes when a citizenry feels itself under scrutiny."[17]

Breaking the Law

"Why does the Constitution have an enumerated powers clause, if the government can do things wildly beyond those powers—such as establish a domestic spying program?" Congressional Representative Ron Paul (R-Tex.) asked.[18]

"In America no one, not even the President is above the law," argued Senator Patrick Leahy. The President and the Justice Department must carry out the laws. "They cannot violate the law or the rights of ordinary Americans," Leahy insisted.[19]

The government has had problems following the law in other areas too. In 2007, the inspector general for the

Department of Justice found widespread problems with the FBI's use of National Security Letters. The letters demand that recipients turn over information for federal investigations.

In thousands of cases, the FBI did not make timely or accurate reports about such letters to Congress, as the law required. In short, the FBI vastly underreported its use of National Security Letters.

Aside from that, the FBI had broken the law on National Security Letters hundreds of times. In about seven hundred cases, the agency got information from telephone companies with "exigent letters," rather than National Security Letters. Basically, the FBI shortcut the process. It got data without going through the steps spelled out in various laws. In dozens of other cases, the FBI lacked valid and current authority to get data, or its demands went beyond what the law allowed.[20]

The report said that the FBI probably could have gotten most of the information anyway if it had followed the law. It also found that the FBI had not acted criminally or deliberately when it broke the law. Often agents had not had proper training or otherwise did not understand the law.

Still, the inspector general told Congress, the FBI may have broken the law up to three thousand times.[21] The fact of so many violations troubled civil rights and privacy advocates. David Sobel at the Electronic Frontier Foundation told *The Washington Post*:

> I think it shows that the bureau has failed to comply with the very minimal requirements that the law imposes on the use of this authority, and underscores the problem that arises when an investigative agency can unilaterally exercise such an invasive power.[22]

Government claims about oversight do not relieve fears, either. As the report on National Security Letters showed, agencies sometimes lie or fail to tell the whole truth.

In other cases, Senator Leahy noted, the executive branch kept materials from Congress on the grounds that they were classified. Congress cannot exercise real oversight if it lacks all the information.[23]

Even when Congress does get information, it may have little ability to curb abuses of power. Howard Dean noted that a special intelligence committee gets regular briefings from the executive branch. However, members cannot legally disclose any details about those briefings.

"What happens if they discover the president has broken the law?" Dean asked.[24] Oversight ability is no good if Congress cannot act in response.

Speaking Out

In running its homeland security programs, the government has sometimes stopped people from speaking out about problems. Sibel Edmonds worked as an FBI translator. She complained to superiors about suspected security leaks and cover-ups. Afterward, the agency fired Edmonds.

With the ACLU's help, Edmonds sued. She claimed the FBI had wrongly fired her for whistle-blowing. Whistle-blowing is calling attention to, or "blowing the whistle on," improper activity.

However, the government said, Edmonds's case involved classified state secrets. The court agreed that the case involved a risk to national security. Thus, the court refused to hear her case. The Supreme Court would not hear an appeal, either. ACLU lawyer Ann Beeson felt the state secrets claim was a ploy to "cut off argument."[25]

In fact, many people feel whistle-blowers perform a valuable public service. Coleen Rowley became one of *Time's* persons of the year in 2002. Rowley wrote a thirteen-page letter criticizing the FBI's handling of local agents' warnings before the September 11 attacks. She delivered it to FBI Director Robert Mueller and to two members of the Senate Intelligence Committee. After someone leaked her letter to

The Patriot Act lets the government get records of the books people check out from public libraries. Critics feel this is an unnecessary government intrusion into people's private lives.

the press, Rowley testified before Congress about agency mismanagement. Rowley kept her job and eventually retired from the FBI. She ran unsuccessfully for Congress in 2006.

Corporate whistle-blowers get protection from dismissal under the Sarbanes-Oxley Act, which became law in 2002. Federal workers' rights are more limited, however. They have lost most court challenges.

Homeland security actions sometimes silence private citizens too. In 2005, FBI agents visited George Christian Windsor of the Connecticut Library Connection. They demanded all records for the library's computer for a date five months earlier. The FBI's National Security Letter also ordered Windsor not to discuss the matter with anyone. Otherwise, he faced criminal penalties.

However, obeying the letter would disclose data about thousands of library users. A state law protected the confidentiality of library patrons' records. Also, freedom to read and learn is closely linked to freedom of speech and association under the First Amendment. The lack of a court-issued warrant presented questions under the Fourth Amendment too.

Windsor talked with the Connecticut Library Consortium's executive board. The librarians decided to challenge the records request. The ACLU filed suit for them in the name of John Doe.

Meanwhile, the national security letter's gag order restricted the librarians. The government mistakenly disclosed their identities. Yet they could not answer press questions. They could not join in public debates about such record requests. They could not even accept an American Library Association award for their defense of intellectual freedom.

After a year, the FBI finally lifted the gag order and dropped its records demand. The librarians could finally speak out. But the FBI could still use national security letters to demand more information without warrants. It issued such letters more than nine thousand times in 2005 alone.[26]

As in the librarians' case, the letters would include gag orders. That is cause to worry, said Windsor's co-plaintiff Janet Nocek: "Because the terrorists tried to scare us all, we should refuse to be scared. The best way to honor those who died on 9/11 is to support our freedoms. If we are quiet, we take away the very thing we are fighting for."[27]

Nocek should know. Her husband died in the September 11 terrorist attacks.

"All the News That's Fit to Print"

News media find themselves under attack too. In some cases, the media have voluntarily curbed their news coverage. For example, the media do not tell about troop movements. In other cases, though, the government has complained.

In June 2006, *The Wall Street Journal, The New York Times,* and *The Los Angeles Times* reported that the government had secretly gotten mounds of financial data from a Belgian group, known as Swift. Records in the Swift database dealt with transactions for thousands of people in America. The CIA ran the program, with oversight from the Treasury Department.

Treasury Department official Stuart Levey argued that the program was "without doubt, a legal and proper use of our authorities." He added that it "has provided us with a unique and powerful window into the operations of terrorist networks."[28]

The government had already said that it would follow terrorists' money trails. Yet many people had not known how sweeping the government's efforts were. "The potential for abuse is enormous," one former counterterrorism official said, even though he supported the program.[29]

The three papers decided that the scope of the government's program was newsworthy and reported it. They did not give any details about leads, transactions, or targets of investigations.

President Bush called the reports "disgraceful." He added that publishing such news "does great harm to the United States of America."[30] Vice President Cheney felt offended.[31] And Peter King (R-N.Y.) of the House Homeland Security Committee felt the government should bring criminal charges. "*The New York Times* is putting its own arrogant, elitist, left-wing agenda before the interests of the American people," he argued.[32]

Some people believed that newspapers threatened America's security by publishing stories about government information-gathering programs. Representative Peter King thought that *The New York Times* had broken the law and should be prosecuted.

The newspapers defended their decisions. Without a grave and overriding reason, *The New York Times* said, its job was to inform the public about important information. In its view, the White House was using the terrorist threat to justify "an extraordinarily powerful executive branch, exempt from the normal checks and balances."[33]

Los Angeles Times editor Dean Baquet noted that the war on terror is a hotly debated topic. "It is our job to publish what we know about the government's role," he said, "to offer the public what it needs to know to participate in that debate."[34]

Free-speech champions say spirited debate is essential in our democracy. In their view, curbing criticism is not patriotic. Rather, it sacrifices one of Americans' dearest freedoms.

A Matter of Principle

When security concerns routinely outweigh individual rights, civil liberties groups say, all Americans suffer. Government over-reaching gives little, if any, protection from proven threats. Instead, it threatens freedom and erodes personal liberties.

In reality, only a minority of Americans have been detained or interrogated under the homeland security program. Security for public transportation, buildings, and events is usually a minor inconvenience. And government surveillance does not interfere with most Americans' daily routine.

Yet civil liberties champions worry about even small encroachments on civil liberties. Otherwise, there is the danger of a "slippery slope." In other words, it becomes easier and easier to justify limits on civil rights. By the time Americans realize what went wrong, it may be too late.

Today, the government might mistreat a small group of suspects. Tomorrow, critics fear, it may limit the rights of criminal defendants in general. Today, the government conducts broad surveillance in the name of safety. Tomorrow, will it spy for political reasons?

Efforts to limit judicial review are a big concern. Civil rights champions also reject the argument that desperate times call for greater presidential power. Americans need our Constitution's protections, especially in times of national emergency. If the government tramples on freedom, they say, then the terrorists will have won.

Saving America From Grave Threats

In other wars, the United States fought specific countries. In the war on terror, no single country is on the "other" side. Terrorist networks reach around the world.

There is no easy way to tell who is a terrorist, either. Most military soldiers wear uniforms. Terrorists blend into their surroundings.

Terrorism also has different targets. Citizens suffer in conventional war, but harming them is not the main goal. Indeed, most people feel soldiers should not attack civilians on purpose.

In contrast, terrorists typically target unarmed civilians.

They aim to kill large numbers of people. They want to instill widespread fear.

"We're battling an enemy committed to an absolute unconditional destruction of our society," former Attorney General John Ashcroft said.[1] The war on terror goes beyond standard law enforcement. And it is more than mere military strategy. It demands all the tools necessary to defend America's way of life.

We Must Find Out

Terrorists today are sophisticated. Besides meetings, letters, and phone calls, they have a host of electronic tools. These include e-mail, blogs, discussion boards, and instant messaging.

Terrorists are masters at masking their actions too. They have been known to hide behind charity organizations. And they have shuffled funds around the globe like financial wizards. As Attorney General Alberto Gonzales told the Senate Judiciary Committee: "Our enemy in this war is no ordinary terrorist organization. Al Qaeda demonstrated on September 11 that it could execute a highly sophisticated operation. . . . And it has promised similar attacks in the future."[2]

America cannot fight terrorism with outdated tools. It must be at least as technologically savvy as the terrorists themselves. And, many people feel, it must use all available means to track down valuable information.

After the September 11 attacks, Congress passed the Patriot Act. Supporters say it is not a broad expansion of the government's powers. Rather, the law updated the way America gathers intelligence in the twenty-first century. That knowledge can help save American lives. The Patriot Act, argues journalist Ronald Kessler, is "simply a tool to prevent terrorism."[3]

Nor should statutes set all the limits on how to fight terror. Supporters of a strong security program want the government to do whatever it must. Homeland security is not like coloring within the lines of a coloring book. It is about protecting the country.

After all, Article II of the Constitution says the president is commander in chief of the armed forces. The United States has been at war before. And presidents have done whatever was necessary to protect the country. Now America is fighting a war on terror.

Terrorists are a threat as great as any foreign country America has fought. Indeed, the president said, the war on terror was why troops went to Afghanistan and then Iraq. The president and executive branch want to track and trap terrorists at home too.

"I believe in a strong, robust executive authority, and I think that the world we live in demands it," Vice President Dick Cheney said in late 2005. In his view, government surveillance did not violate civil liberties. Rather, Cheney said, "It has saved thousands of lives."[4]

> **America cannot fight terrorism with outdated tools. It must be at least as technologically savvy as the terrorists themselves.**

In the same vein, President Bush admitted in 2005 that he had authorized the NSA to do some electronic surveillance without FISA warrants. But he felt that was "fully consistent with [his] constitutional responsibilities and authorities." Also, to prevent against abuses, the president's office reviewed the program approximately every forty-five days. The president concluded:

> This authorization [for electronic surveillance] is a vital tool in our war against the terrorists. It is critical to saving American lives. The American people expect me to do everything in my power under our laws and Constitution to protect them and their civil liberties. And that is exactly what I will continue to do, so long as I'm President of the United States.[5]

Senator Trent Lott (R-Miss.) agreed. "I want my security first," he said. "I'll deal with all the details after that."[6] Indeed, many Americans want their president to act decisively.

"In a time of national emergency, I expect the President to take such actions to protect our Nation," wrote Senator Mike DeWine (R-Ohio), "even if those actions are not specifically authorized by statute." After newspapers published information about the NSA's surveillance of international phone calls, DeWine proposed a law to ratify the program. He felt the bill would help "avoid a divisive debate in Congress and throughout our Nation."[7] A different bill, passed by Congress in 2007, in fact expanded government surveillance powers, at least temporarily.

Supporters of the government's actions also point to a 2001 resolution from Congress. It told the president to use "all necessary and appropriate force" to fight terrorism.[8] That would include surveillance work both inside and outside the country. Such work is "a fundamental incident of the use of military force," argued the Justice Department's Office of Legislative Affairs.[9]

Several Supreme Court justices probably agree. Opinions in a 2004 case said that the resolution was grounds to hold an American who had fought for the Taliban in Afghanistan. By analogy, homeland supporters want a broad range for government action.[10]

Mort Zuckerman of *U.S. News & World Report* has argued that America must respond to possible threats in the timeliest way. As President Abraham Lincoln once said, "Must a government, of necessity, be too strong for the liberties of its own people, or too weak to maintain its own existence?"[11]

Broad government power makes sense to supporters of a strong security program. They do not want to limit antiterrorism programs. Rather, the government should cast as wide a net as possible.

Think about efforts to track terrorists' money. The government has identified certain charities as avenues for terrorist financing. That has slowed the flow of money to al-Qaeda and other groups.

Other efforts have been more difficult, however, because of waiting periods before worldwide freezes of assets take effect. The more international cooperation the United States can get, the better it can curb the flow of funds to terrorists.

In any case, the question is not just whether the government can "starve the terrorists of money." As the 9/11 Commission noted, "The government has recognized that information about terrorist money helps us to understand their networks, search them out, and disrupt their operations."[12]

President George W. Bush believes that the government should do whatever it must to defeat terrorism. He believes the steps his administration have taken are constitutional and do not unduly limit civil liberties.

Some of the government's surveillance work has gathered private records. Yet sometimes such data is not really secret anyway. Some people felt shocked when news sources said the government used the Swift database. Yet commercial databases sell information to credit-card companies, financial institutions, or marketers all the time. Why shouldn't the government also use such sources to protect America? Homeland security supporters see no reason not to use such tools.

Civil rights groups worry about the large quantities of data that the government collects. However, a process called data mining can spot signs of possible terrorist activity. It can show links that may lead to saving lives. Homeland security supporters feel that is good.

Valdis Krebs's work gives one example of how phone bills, financial records, and other data can help detect terrorists. After 2001, Krebs, an analyst with Organet.com, used computer programs to study connections between two men involved in the U.S.S. *Cole* bombing in 2000. The analysis turned up links to Muhammad Atta, a hijacker in the September 11 attacks.

Yes, looking for terrorists through data mining is somewhat like looking for a needle in the proverbial haystack. Unless agencies can uncover that needle, though, the country could suffer another massive attack. According to DHS Secretary Michael Chertoff, the United States' best defense against terrorism is to gather information and to act on it as soon as possible:

> The best tool in dealing with homegrown terrorists is intelligence—collection, analysis and sharing. That is our early warning system. The sooner we detect a plot or a threat, the better our chances of dismantling it before it becomes operational.[13]

Only the Guilty Have to Worry

The government has a massive surveillance and intelligence program. Nonetheless, supporters say, that program is targeted at terrorists. Despite dire claims by civil rights groups, ordinary citizens have nothing to fear. President Bush stressed this in May 2006 when he talked about government review of phone records:

> Al Qaeda is our enemy, and we want to know their plans. . . . We're not mining or trolling through the personal lives of millions of innocent Americans. Our efforts are focused on links to al Qaeda and their known affiliates. So far we've been very successful in preventing another attack on our soil.[14]

When the government collects vast amounts of data, it really is not interested in the calls ordinary Americans make to friends and relatives. Nor does it care which Web sites most people visit on the Internet. The government may get that information as part of its massive intelligence-gathering activities. But no one in the government really has time to tinker with such details. Too much is at stake in the war on terror.

More importantly, America values its tradition of civil liberties. Compared with other times when America has faced threats, complaints from civil rights groups today seem minor. The government's homeland security measures since the September 11 attacks "pale in comparison" to what earlier presidents did during wartime, noted historian Jay Winik. In his view, the Bush administration's actions immediately after the attacks showed "remarkable restraint."[15]

Indeed, agency leaders are sensitive to civil rights issues. Thus, DHS Secretary Michael Chertoff has told Congress he is "dead set" against targeting people for investigation based on their religion. "It strikes the fabric of our own country and what we believe in our Constitution and our civil liberties to single out people based upon their religion," Chertoff said.[16]

The government has procedures to review any claims of abuse. Both the DHS and Department of Justice have inspector generals. Their job is to investigate complaints.

The Government Accountability Office and congressional committees also conduct reviews as necessary.

Frequent review and oversight protect against possible abuse. For example, the president's office reviewed the program for monitoring international phone calls without FISA warrants every forty-five days. Additionally, the executive branch briefed congressional committees. Attorney General Alberto Gonzales argued that such safeguards should reassure Americans that the government is acting in their best interests.[17]

While some critics say government actions are extreme, supporters say they get the job done. Techniques for questioning terror suspects have been rougher than those used on ordinary criminals. Nonetheless, Vice President Dick Cheney argued, "We have to work . . . the dark side, if you will."[18]

"Altogether, information from terrorists in CIA custody has played a role in the capture or questioning of nearly every senior al Qaeda member or associate detained by the United States and its allies," President Bush said. "Were it not for this program," he added, "our intelligence community believes that al Qaeda and its allies would have succeeded in launching another attack against the American homeland."[19]

Many members of the public agree. In one 2005 survey, nearly three fourths of those questioned felt that torture claims hurt America's image. Yet 58 percent said they would support torture if it could prevent an attack.[20]

While it is tough on terrorists, the government insists it respects basic rights. For example, the Military Commissions Act of 2006 has terms that forbid grave breaches of the Geneva Conventions. The provisions came from compromise with congressional leaders who opposed torture. Among them was Senator John McCain, who suffered torture firsthand during the Vietnam War.

"There's no doubt that the integrity and letter and spirit of the Geneva Conventions have been preserved," McCain said

Michael Chertoff, secretary of the Department of Homeland Security, says that getting information and acting on it quickly is the only way to win the war on terror.

shortly before Congress passed the law. "The agreement that we've entered into gives the president the tools he needs to continue to fight the war on terror and bring these evil people to justice."[21]

Most importantly, President Bush said, the law would save American lives. "We will protect our country and our people," he vowed.[22]

America Needs a United Front

Spirited debate is a big part of America's political tradition. Nonetheless, the country has pulled together in times of great crisis, such as World War II. Supporters of a strong homeland security program say the war on terror is another major crisis. They do not want media reports or public criticism to undermine government efforts.

After the September 11 attacks, al-Qaeda leader Osama bin Laden released several videos. The films had harsh words against the United States. The government worried that the videos would inflame hatred against America. The messages might also contain code words to touch off more terrorist attacks.

Leaders from five major news outlets spoke with then national security adviser Condoleezza Rice. As a result, they limited their coverage of bin Laden's videos. "After hearing Dr. Rice, we're not going to step on the land mines she was talking about," remarked CNN chairman Walter Isaacson.[23]

News coverage about military efforts abroad is also sensitive. Media outlets may well want to show coffins of deceased soldiers coming back from Iraq. However, the Pentagon bans such television coverage. It says this is out of respect for "the privacy of the families during their time of greatest loss and grief."[24]

Newspapers and television stations did show some of those images in 2004, after a reporter got photos through a Freedom of Information Act request. (The Freedom of Information Act lets citizens get various documents from government agencies.)

The media outlets said they were merely covering the news. They felt the public deserved to know the costs of the war. Pentagon supporters complained the media was making a political statement. In any case, the Pentagon order stayed in place.

Media attention about surveillance bothered supporters of the government's homeland security program. The government claimed it had acted properly. Yet it still had to spend time and resources answering allegations.

Supporters say that time could have been better spent tracking down terrorists. "Rather than allow our intelligence professionals to maintain a laser focus on the terrorists, we are once again mired in a debate about what our intelligence community may or may not be doing," complained Representative Peter Hoekstra (R-Mich.).[25]

More seriously, government supporters say, releasing details about government programs can tip off terrorists. When *The New York Times* revealed the NSA's spying on international calls and e-mails, President Bush objected.

"This program is so sensitive and so important that if information gets out to how we run it or how we operate it, it'll help the enemy," Bush said. "Why tell the enemy what we're doing?"[26]

To a large extent, the government's actions in tracking terrorist subjects are classified. Even if the media can lawfully publish leaked information, government supporters say that is often unwise. Attempts to boost circulation or ratings numbers are not good reasons to jeopardize homeland security.

Politics should not motivate the media either, say government supporters. More than ever, they feel, America needs a united front against terrorists. Critical news reports suggest Americans might not be willing to persevere in fighting terrorism at home and abroad.

Thus, former Secretary of Defense Donald Rumsfeld felt it was wrong for retired generals to criticize America's actions in

Iraq. "They are encouraging the enemy to fight on, believing we will ultimately surrender," he said.[27]

Conservative commentator Pat Robertson has even suggested it is treason to disagree with the president as America's commander in chief.[28] Robertson's view of the law was wrong. Yet some people agree that too much criticism of the government is unpatriotic.

Others feel that "bad-mouthing" the government sends the wrong message to troops abroad.[29] Of course, one can disagree with the government on some things and yet support the efforts

Commissioner W. Ralph Basham of U.S. Customs and Border Protection speaks to border patrol agents and National Guard troops in Tucson, Arizona. Many people believe that government agencies should not be limited in their ability to enforce the law and thwart terrorists.

and sacrifices of America's soldiers. For many people, though, the issue is much more emotional than logical.

As a separate matter, people who leak information to the media may be committing a crime. The First Amendment may let news outlets publish information once they get it. However, the Constitution does not shield people who have a duty to keep classified information secret.

Protecting information from disclosure is part of the job for many people. When they get a security clearance and take a job, they agree to keep information confidential. Not everything they deal with may be super secret. But it is not the employee's job to decide what can or cannot be told to others.

If someone has a problem with keeping secrets, he or she can simply find work outside the government. Yes, employees may find problems within the government. However, they can follow the rules to bring any issues to the attention of their supervisors or others within their agency.

An individual may not like the way an issue gets resolved. But, government supporters would say, going outside the agency is not the answer. Such whistle-blowers may feel like they are being heroes. When they do not have the whole picture, though, misguided action could jeopardize important government programs. Homeland security supporters say that could be disastrous.

Striking a Balance

In his book *All the Laws But One*, former Chief Justice William H. Rehnquist argued that limits on civil liberties make sense during wartime. Civil liberties do not exist in a vacuum. Rather, they are rights that citizens have, and citizens owe their allegiance to their government.

Actions that threaten the nation can thus properly limit personal freedoms. Rehnquist wrote:

> In any civilized society the most important task is achieving a proper balance between freedom and order. In wartime, reason and history both suggest that this balance shifts to some degree in favor of order—in favor of the government's ability to deal with conditions that threaten the national well-being.[30]

Former Attorney General Francis Biddle put it more bluntly when he said, "The Constitution has not greatly bothered any wartime President."[31] Biddle served under Franklin Roosevelt during World War II.

The idea that national security trumps concerns about civil liberties goes back to ancient times. As Roman politician and author Cicero put it, "*Inter arma silent leges*"—"In times of war, laws are silent."[32]

Rehnquist's argument is most persuasive when the American public perceives a direct danger. Rhetoric—the language used in speeches—often plays up this concern. Speeches by President Bush and others often contain reminders about the September 11 attacks. They talk about the "war on terror."[33] Even the term *homeland security* evokes notions of protecting one's home from danger.

Such rhetoric often works too. A 2005 study by the Pew Research Center found that George W. Bush won a second term as president for one main reason: "The electorate judged him to be the stronger leader at a time when Americans feel threatened by terrorism."[34] Boston University professor Andrew Bacevich agrees that "scaremongering" has helped candidates for decades.[35] Appeals to Americans' worries about safety and security will likely play a big part in future elections as well.

In debates about civil liberties, the government has not publicly pushed the position that sacrificing some rights is a proper trade-off in times of war. Instead, it prefers to argue that its actions are justified. This happened, for example, when groups complained about electronic surveillance without FISA warrants.

Alternatively, the government has carved out exceptions from the general rule. Thus, it wanted to reclassify people held under suspicion of terror as enemy combatants. Then they could treat them differently from regular citizens.

These approaches let the government avoid any admission that it acted outside the law or curtailed citizens' rights. For one thing, political leaders may not want to admit that life now is different from the business-as-usual situation. After all, voters may switch to the other political party if they fear the present leaders are not really protecting them.

Moreover, voters may feel uncomfortable if the government admits it is curtailing civil liberties. That discomfort increases if people fear that their own freedoms are in danger.

Rehnquist was right when he wrote that society needs a proper balance between order and freedom. And history supports his view that wartime worries often shift that balance in favor of government actions. Nevertheless, America's elected leaders must tread carefully. Otherwise, voters may decide to strike a different balance by supporting other candidates in the next election.

Homeland security affects millions of Americans every year, as well as international travelers. To work well, procedures must be practical, yet thorough. However, even the best programs cannot stop all terrorists.

Terrorism is not the only problem America faces, either. The country must balance homeland security concerns with other priorities. Inevitably, conflicts arise.

Dollars and Sense?

Homeland security costs money—and lots of it. Overall spending for homeland security exceeds $40 billion annually. This includes money spent by DHS. It also includes activities by some other agencies, such as the Department of Defense and the FBI.[1]

Much of the money pays employees' salaries. Additionally, funds go to companies for products and services. Money also goes to states and local governments, for grants, personnel training, and so on.

Decisions about who gets those dollars matter a lot to state and local economies. Companies jockey with one another to bid for business. State and local governments compete for resources too.

Common sense says America should spend homeland security dollars where the greatest risks are. Determining those risks is not so easy, though. Consider the National Asset Database.

Started in 1998, the database aims to identify key resources. The database includes national monuments and government buildings. It also has energy resources, water supplies, transportation hubs, and health facilities. Some businesses are on the list too.

In 2003, the list had 160 sites. By 2006, it had more than 77,000 sites. From states' viewpoint, more sites might mean more funds. Thus, they added listings. Facilities went into the database with little DHS review.

Many sites were clearly important. In 2006, the list included 224 national monuments and icons, or symbols. It also had 335 petroleum pipelines and 178 nuclear power plants.

However, the DHS inspector general's office found that the database also had many listings that really did not belong. Such sites included an ice-cream parlor, a casket company, a brewery, and more than thirteen hundred casinos.[2]

Indiana had 8,591 sites, versus 5,687 for New York and 3,212 for California. "A travel stop, a petting zoo, a roller rink are sites," complained Senator Charles Schumer (D-N.Y.). "But then the Statue of Liberty and the Brooklyn Bridge aren't?"[3]

"I've been trying to figure out why we're on the terrorist watch list," roller rink owner Marg Wall told Comedy Central's *The Daily Show*. "I really don't think that we are that important."[4]

All joking aside, the database did not identify clear national priorities in case of an attack. That was a serious shortcoming.

DHS replied that the list should show all potential targets. Congressional efforts to make DHS revise the list failed in 2006. Without other action in Congress, the agency may continue the same approach.

Americans on the Move

After September 11, America tightened its flight security. Airplanes now have reinforced cockpit doors. Thousands of armed federal air marshals police flights. Passengers get checked against expanded terrorist watch lists. Luggage screening by TSA personnel has caught more than 12 million forbidden items. As a result, DHS says air travel is "safer now than ever before."[5]

While all passengers go through metal detectors and have their luggage screened, some travelers go through additional security checks. These include pat-downs or "puffer" machine scans of their bodies, plus hand inspection of carry-on luggage. ("Puffers" blow air at someone and analyze it for traces of certain chemicals.)

Flying one way, changing flights unexpectedly, or paying cash for a ticket can trigger the scrutiny. Other times, TSA picks people at random. People sometimes feel hassled for no reason. Or they question whether random searches will really trap terrorists.

On the other hand, smart terrorists would use people who do not attract suspicion. Random searches also test how thorough the general screening is.

Sadly, airport screening has been nowhere near as thorough

as it could be. In 2005, the Government Accountability Office found that airport screening for weapons was little better than in 2001. In 2006, investigators got ingredients to make bombs past screeners at twenty-one airports.[6] In another study, guns and bombs got past airport screeners in at least twenty cases at Newark Liberty International Airport.[7]

Tests are one thing. Actual security failures are worse. In 2007, an employee smuggled fourteen guns onto a commercial plane. In another case, a nine-year-old boy snuck onto planes in Seattle and Arizona. Airport authorities finally caught him in Dallas.[8] Fortunately, neither incident involved terrorists. But they offer little comfort to fliers who worry about safety.

Shorter security lines for some passengers raise more issues. Various airports use them for first class and frequent fliers with lots of miles. Other airports have registered traveler programs. Passengers pay an annual fee ($100–$200) and submit to private companies' background checks. In return, they use faster lines at airports.

Is "speedy security" fair? Registered travelers actually go through more security. After all, they have background checks. And travelers, not the TSA, pay the costs. Yet the TSA was set up because private security firms did not stop the September 11 hijackers. Critics may thus worry whether private security companies should play a role again. Also, some say, privilege should not play a part in public safety.

Gaps in airport screening raise more criticisms. After a 2006 threat about liquid bombs, the TSA limited the ability of passengers to carry liquids onto planes. The government had known about the possibility of liquid explosives since 1995. Yet as late as 2006, airports still did not have reliable technology for detecting them.

Meanwhile, tons of cargo still went on airplanes without X-ray screening. House Representative Edward Markey (D-Mass.) said this was like "leaving your back door wide open"

The Massachusetts Bay Transportation Authority has high-tech systems to track developments in the bus and rail systems in and around Boston. America's mass transit systems now face the challenge of trying to prevent terrorist attacks as well.

to a possible terrorist attack.[9] Everyone wants airlines to run smoothly. But Americans want to be safe as well.

More controversy centers on flight watch lists. Edward Allen's name came up, for example, but the four-year-old obviously was not a terrorist. Dozens of David Nelsons have had hours of airport delays when their names came up too. Among them were company executives, a retired building manager, an actor, and a federal court judge. Even Senator Ted Kennedy has been subject to extra scrutiny.

No one knows the total number of mistaken identification cases. A 2006 report by the Government Accountability Office suggested that the number is in the thousands, though. In one two-year period, about half the cases reviewed by the Terrorist Screening Center were false alarms. The person "caught" was not the suspected terrorist in the government's records.

Some people caught up by the watch lists have felt frustrated. Others have felt scared. "I've had one officer tell another to put me in handcuffs and take me away," said David Fathi, a lawyer in Washington State.[10]

The TSA agreed that its procedures need improvement.[11] Meanwhile, the ACLU has filed several lawsuits for people who were delayed. At least one lawsuit has settled. Others remain pending.

Of course, airlines are not the only way to travel. Every day, millions of Americans take trains, subways, buses, cars, and ferries. Terrorists attack those types of transportation too.

In 2006, for example, approximately one hundred eighty people died and more than seven hundred suffered injuries after a bomb exploded on a train in Mumbai, India. Bomb attacks on London's Underground and a bus killed nearly sixty people in 2005. Terrorist bombs exploded on Russian passenger and subway trains in 2004 and 2005. Bombs in Madrid killed nearly two hundred commuter train passengers in 2004.

Mass transit systems in the United States have had bomb scares too. One event threatened to blow up twenty New York subway trains. Another threat warned that a bomb might flood the Holland Tunnel and lower Manhattan.

In another case, a jury convicted a Pakistani immigrant for plotting to blow up New York's Herald Square subway station. And even before the September 11 bombings, the Washington Metro had more than a dozen bomb threats.

DHS seminars train mass transit workers so they can try to prevent attacks. Transit authorities take other steps too. In

Boston, transit workers and police ask riders to report suspicious packages or activity. In Washington, remote-control robotics inspect suspicious packages.

Some safety programs are more intrusive. New York transit police have made random searches of passengers' bags. In 2006, a federal court upheld the program.

In another case, a fifty-year-old woman would not show identification when her public bus went through Denver's large federal office center. The federal government later dropped the charges. The city also considered ways to reroute buses and avoid federal land.

In short, courts will uphold reasonable public safety programs. Nevertheless, most cities and states want to avoid huge holdups or hassles. After all, commuters are also voters.

Border Crossings

More than half a billion people legally cross America's borders every year. Millions also enter illegally. Estimates say that more than 11 million people are in the United States unlawfully.[12] Many of them come to escape poverty.

The pros and cons of immigration policies are beyond the scope of this book. Nevertheless, some people sneaking into the country may threaten Americans' safety. That is a matter of homeland security.

To the north, the United States and Canada share 5,526 miles of borders. This includes 1,539 miles between Alaska and Canada. To the south, the Mexican border measures 1,952 miles.

The United States also has more than twelve thousand miles of coastline. The U.S. Coast Guard patrols the nation's coastal waters. U.S. Customs and Border Protection (CBP) is the overall guardian of America's borders.

CBP's Secure Border Initiative aims to keep terrorists out by cutting down on all illegal crossings. The program will eventually cover six thousand miles of border. Its first phase focuses on the Tucson area, including remote sensors for a "virtual fence."[13]

Border protection plans call for real fences too. In 2006, Congress voted to build a seven-hundred-mile-long fence along the Mexican-U.S. border, for a cost of $1.2 billion. The law's provisions let DHS use discretion, though. Thus, it may invest in lighting, radar, cameras, and other tools.

"That's what the people of this country want," President Bush said when he signed the bill. "They want to know that we're modernizing the border so we can better secure the border."[14]

Critics wonder whether any fence can really keep terrorists out. America's immigration problems will remain too. CBP also announced it would add about 50 percent more agents, bringing the total to eighteen thousand people. Critics hope the extra people will be trained and qualified.[15]

Who gets to enter the United States? As in airports, CBP uses watch lists. Beyond that, citizens of most other countries need a visa. (As of 2006, people from about twenty countries—mostly in Europe—were exempt from the visa requirement.)

Visas help the government control and monitor entry. They also make it easier to prescreen people. Since 2001, the government has investigated people more thoroughly and tracked them better inside the United States. However, stepped-up security procedures have led to delays for foreign students, workers, and visitors.

Better procedures eventually cut down on most delays. Nonetheless, delays deter some people from work and study in the United States. Even several years after the September 11 attacks, some scientists turned down jobs rather than put up with security hassles.[16]

Politics may be at work too. The University of Notre Dame hired Tariq Ramadan to teach Islamic studies and philosophy.

A CBP agent checks a traveler's documents before allowing entry into the United States. Airport security and border enforcement have become much stricter in recent years.

In 2004, however, the United States revoked the Swiss citizen's visa. Ramadan had criticized the war in Iraq.

The ACLU and several scholarly groups sued. They raised arguments about intellectual freedom and American students' rights under the First Amendment to hear different viewpoints. In 2006, a federal court ordered the government to either grant Ramadan a visa or justify not doing so. Meanwhile, though, Ramadan had given up his post.[17]

Visa issues also delayed Aymara Indian scholar Waskar Ari from starting his job at the University of Nebraska-Lincoln (UNL). When Ari made a short visit to his home in Bolivia, the government canceled his old student visa. Meanwhile, it held up Ari's new work visa. No one would say why.

The American Historical Association and officials at UNL and Georgetown University all asked the State Department to grant Ari's visa. Ari was a political moderate, not a terrorist. Indeed, a grant from the U.S. government had let Ari earn his doctorate degree from Georgetown University. American students would benefit from his insights in Latin American studies.

After nearly two years, Ari finally received the visa, but only after UNL had filed suit on his behalf. "My ordeal lasted more than two years and I am glad it ended," Ari said soon after arriving to teach at UNL in 2007.[18]

Security hurdles will remain high for both citizens and noncitizens. Now almost everyone entering the United States needs a passport. (Some exceptions may apply.)

Getting around within the United States will get harder too. A 2005 law set up the Real ID program. American drivers must prove their identities at license renewal time. The law's supporters hope it will prevent another situation like that in 2001. Most of the September 11 hijackers had valid driver's licenses.

Civil liberties groups say ordinary citizens will face hassles if they need four forms of identification to get a driver's license. Beyond that, proposed rules called for licenses to have machine readable code. The Privacy Rights Clearinghouse and ACLU feel such features could subject millions of Americans to easy identity theft.[19] Identity thieves use other people's information to get credit or buy things fraudulently. When victims finally find out, correcting problems may take hundreds of hours.

Real ID worries states too. As of 2007, lawmakers in Maine, Washington, and several other states had passed resolutions rejecting Real ID. Lawmakers in those states wanted federal funding and better privacy protections for consumers. A bill to that effect was pending in 2007.[20]

Nevertheless, government officials face a tough job. No one wants terrorists to slip through security again the way they did in 2001. As Department of Homeland Security spokesperson Valerie Smith said:

> The mission of the Department of Homeland Security is to protect Americans from terrorism and the mission of Customs and Border Protection is to prevent terrorists and their weapons from entering our country. It is incumbent upon Customs officers to be right each and every time. Terrorists only have to get it right once.[21]

Preparing for the Worst

Chemical, biological, and nuclear attacks could kill millions more Americans than traditional bombs could. Even before 2001, the government began planning for that possibility. Now the need is becoming more urgent.

Public health authorities have set up response plans in case of attacks. Meanwhile, agencies work on ways to diagnose potential disease outbreaks more quickly.

For example, DHS's BioWatch regularly checks air samples in urban areas. Public health authorities could then step into action more quickly to prevent or treat disease. Other programs aim to boost supplies of vaccines and medicines.

Public health authorities may be preparing for possible attacks, but most ordinary citizens are not. One DHS publication warned: "We must have the tools and plans in place to make it on our own, at least for a period of time, no matter where we are when disaster strikes. Just like having a working smoke detector, preparing for the unexpected makes sense. Get ready now."[22]

General recommendations for emergency supplies of food, water, flashlights, and first-aid materials tracked those from groups like the American Red Cross. Beyond that, DHS told people to have drop cloths and duct tape handy. In case of an attack, they could seal off windows and doors.[23]

Thousands of people stocked up on bottled water, batteries, and duct tape. Others questioned the wisdom of the government's advice. Sealing off rooms seemed like overkill. Plus, it would limit the air supply. In a real attack, such measures might make little difference anyway.

Public health authorities may be preparing for possible attacks, but most ordinary citizens are not.

On one level, the government's recommendations reassure some citizens. By making a survival kit, they feel as if they are doing something for their own safety. Other people wonder whether the government is really prepared if its best advice is to buy duct tape.

Americans felt even less confidence after hurricanes struck America's Gulf Coast in 2005. Hurricane Katrina claimed more than one thousand lives across Louisiana, Mississippi, and Alabama. Its damage estimates ranged between $40 and $60 billion. Hurricane Rita caused even more damage just a few weeks later.[24]

The hurricanes were natural disasters, not terrorist acts. Nonetheless, they were the first major test after 2001 for the government's disaster-preparedness program. At first, President Bush praised Michael Brown, head of the Federal Emergency Management Association (FEMA), for the agency's response work: "Brownie, you're doing a heck of a job. The FEMA Director is working 24—they're working 24 hours a day."[25]

Thousands of people disagreed. Refugees at the New Orleans Convention Center could not get enough food or water to drink. Sick people could not get medical attention.

"The convention center is unsanitary and unsafe, and we are running out of supplies for the 15,000 to 20,000 people," complained Mayor Ray Nagin.[26] Questions of racism arose too,

A search-and-rescue team brings storm victims to safety after Hurricane Katrina. The U.S. government was severely criticized for being unprepared for the problems posed by the disaster.

since most people left in the city were people of color. Media outlets severely criticized FEMA, DHS, and the Bush Administration.

In response, Michael Chertoff, the Director of DHS, said that the New Orleans floods "exceeded the foresight of planners." At least thirty-two hours before the hurricane hit land, though, Brown and other federal officials had news that the storm would likely cause widespread flooding. "They knew that this one was different," said Max Mayfield of the National Hurricane Center.[27]

William Hartung of the World Policy Institute argued that America should adjust its priorities to deal with the most pressing threats.[28] Hurricanes and other natural disasters are more likely to affect large numbers of people than terrorist attacks. The government should plan and be ready for them.

Congress responded by boosting FEMA's budget by about 10 percent annually for three years. It also made FEMA more independent within DHS. Senator Joseph Lieberman (D-Conn.) said the changes should get rid of separation of "those who are supposed to prepare for disasters from those who are supposed to respond to them."[29]

The Katrina catastrophe also drew criticism from those who worry about homeland security. As DHS Secretary Michael Chertoff admitted, "Whether it's a natural disaster or a disaster caused by a terrorist, our response is often going to be the same."[30] People would need food, shelter, escape routes, and emergency services.

DHS had failed its first real trial for disaster preparedness. Indeed, terrorist attacks occur with less warning than hurricanes. Thus, the government's goof-ups could even be worse.

Where Do We Go from Here?

Weighing the costs and benefits of homeland security is not easy. Critics like journalist James Bovard feel the government has far "more strikeouts than hits" in the war on terror.[1] Government supporters say it has done an outstanding job of protecting America.

Are We Winning the War on Terror?

The United States has made hundreds of arrests in the war on terror. Yet those arrests sometimes spotlight both flaws and successes in homeland security.

For example, Zacarias Moussaoui went to prison for life for

his part in the September 11 conspiracy. However, his August 2001 arrest did not stop the attacks.

In early 2003, a federal court sent Richard Reid to prison for life. Reid failed in his attempt to blow up an American Airlines jet. But tighter security did not spot Reid's shoe bomb. "Basically, I got on the plane with the bomb," Reid said. Passengers stopped him from lighting the bomb.[2]

In 2006, the FBI said that it had foiled a plot to blow up mass transit tunnels linking New York and New Jersey. FBI Assistant Director Mark Mehrson said the threat was "the real deal." However, another official told *The Washington Post* that the plot was just "jihadi bravado"—more talk than action.[3]

Also in 2006, the government arrested seven people who plotted to blow up the Sears Tower in Chicago. Attorney General Alberto Gonzales praised "our commitment to preventing terrorism through energetic law enforcement efforts." Much of the evidence came from an FBI informant, however. Defense lawyer Nathan Clark argued that the government was trying "to set these people up."[4]

Another arrest stopped a plan to attack the Capitol and World Bank in Washington. The plan did not pose an immediate threat. However, U.S. Attorney David Nahmias said, "We no longer wait until a bomb is built and ready to explode."[5]

The government has also adjusted threat advisory levels and changed security measures when new developments happen. For example, alert levels rose after the government learned that terrorists planned to use liquid bombs on international flights. British authorities arrested a group for that plot in 2006.

Not all actions to thwart terrorism lead to headlines. Some of the biggest coups in the war on terror may never make the news. Much of the government's antiterrorism work is classified. It does not want to tip off terrorists about its work. Undercover agents need to maintain cover too. Yet government supporters say such "silent victories" do occur.

"The bottom line is that there have been no terrorist attacks in the United States since 9/11," said Senate Majority Leader Bill Frist (R-Tenn.) in 2006.[6] (More accurately, there had been few successful attacks since September 11. The 2001 anthrax mailings count as terrorist activity.)

Other supporters used the small number of attacks to argue for even stronger security. "We haven't been attacked in five years," noted former New York Mayor Rudolph Giuliani on the fifth anniversary of the September 11 attacks. "I thank God we haven't," he added. "But we have to prepare for it."[7]

DHS Secretary Michael Chertoff made a similar point in September 2006. He noted that "perfect security" could only come at "an astronomical cost to our liberty and our prosperity." Yet he argued for a strong and vigilant homeland security program: "This is a struggle that will be with us in years to come, and it is a struggle we will win as long as we remain steadfast, dedicated, and balanced in the approach that we take."[8]

Much of the government's antiterrorism work is classified, so some of the biggest coups in the war on terror may never make the news.

The government may not deserve full credit for any absence of attacks. Few terrorists attacked America in the five years before 2001, noted political science professor John Mueller at The Ohio State University. Certainly, terrorism is a serious problem. However, Mueller said, officials may have exaggerated al-Qaeda's numbers, resources, and abilities.[9]

Other critics say America is not doing enough. Senator Joseph Biden (D-Del.) warned against taking "false comfort from the fact" that al-Qaeda had not made another attack on American soil in the five years after 2001.

"Our enemies are patient," Biden told the National Press Club.[10] He proposed hiring one thousand more FBI agents and fifty thousand additional police officers nationwide. He would fund the $50 billion program with higher taxes on Americans earning more than $1 million per year.

Officials discuss a border patrol initiative in Arizona at a press conference in Washington, D.C. Opinions differ on how successful the war on terror has been.

Al-Qaeda may be even more dangerous now than in 2001, said Bruce Riedel at the Brookings Institution. In his view, American foreign policy has let al-Qaeda strengthen and expand its bases. As a result, the United States may be more vulnerable than ever.[11]

Government bureaucracy also causes concern. The Markle Foundation studies how technology can address critical needs in national security and health. Among other things, the group reported, DHS could not adequately handle real-time operations. It did not guard against potential breakdowns in

The Homeland Security Advisory System

The Department of Homeland Security uses a color-coded Threat Level System. Its purpose is to communicate with public safety officials and the public at large about current threats and the likelihood of attack. The higher the threat level, the more guarded DHS wants people to be.

communication. Also, DHS and other federal agencies engaged in turf wars—battles about who should do which jobs.[12]

Creation of the DHS was supposed to unify homeland security work. Instead, critics said, the bureaucracy was as unwieldy as ever. "They have created a completely illogical system," noted Seth Jones of the RAND Corporation, which does lots of defense research.[13]

Representative Zoe Lofgren (D-Calif.) had similar feelings. "If the American people knew how little has been done, they would be outraged," she complained.[14]

Technology is often outdated too. Evan Kohlmann runs a Global Terror Alert Web site. He noted that terrorist groups excel at using the Internet for propaganda, communication, recruitment, and fund-raising. Meanwhile, some American government offices were still using dial-up Internet connections. Also, the government did not use online resources effectively.[15]

America needs human skills to trap terrorists too. Daniel Byman of Georgetown University's Security Studies Program wants to see more FBI agents with skills in Arabic. He feels that would give them important cultural knowledge.[16] Beyond this, one would hope all people working in homeland security would be well qualified for their jobs.

Clark Kent Ervin at the Aspen Institute notes more glaring

The U.S. government has encouraged people to put together supplies for emergencies, including terrorist attacks. Some people are doubtful about their usefulness.

gaps. The Department of Homeland Security has made it harder than ever for terrorists to enter America. Yet determined people still can sneak in.

Ervin also argues that the homeland security program has been wasteful and inefficient. American taxpayers bear the costs. Meanwhile, the country runs the risk that dangerous terrorists will strike.[17]

Too Much Power?

The government says it is watching out for America's interests. Yet critics complain that no one is really watching over the government. One concern is expanding presidential power.

"I believe in this day and age, it's important that we have a strong presidency," Vice President Dick Cheney told *The Wall Street Journal.* Yes, the Constitution imposes some restraints. However, Cheney felt the president should have more power.[18]

President Bush took a similar view when news broke about the government's domestic surveillance program. The president felt that he had inherent power to authorize the NSA's actions.

Critics reject such arguments. They want all the checks and balances for each branch of government that the Constitution provides.

In 2006, President Bush claimed that the NSA only wire-tapped people with links to terrorism. However, he would not let a judge review the case. Senator Russ Feingold (D-Wis.) felt that was wrong:

> Our job is not to stand up and cheer when the President breaks the law. Our job is to stand up and demand accountability, to stand up and check the power of an out-of-control Executive Branch.[19]

A Congressional Research Service memorandum found it "difficult to imagine" that the Constitution's framers would forbid the federal government from foreign intelligence collection. Nonetheless, it found that the Justice Department was on shaky grounds in arguing that the president had inherent authority for domestic spying.[20]

Congress had passed various laws, including FISA and the Patriot Act, that said when and how the government could conduct surveillance. For the executive branch to go beyond those laws seemed sketchy at best. At worst, critics said, the executive branch was breaking the law.

Former White House Counsel John Dean felt the Bush administration was pushing executive power further than any earlier president. Dean felt that went against Supreme Court decisions on the relationship between the president and Congress.[21] Moreover, if Congress could not restrict the president's actions on national security, what limits would there be?

Critics likewise questioned whether the 2001 congressional resolution authorizing force against terrorism justified the executive branch's acts. Senator Lindsey Graham (R-SC) voted for the resolution. However, he never meant to give the president "carte blanche" (a blank check) for domestic spying or other activities.[22]

An ACLU lawsuit argued that the government's domestic spying program "violates longstanding separation of powers principles."[23] In 2006, a federal district court ruled in favor of the ACLU's position. It held that the government's spying violated the rights to free speech and privacy and went against separation of powers under the Constitution. However, the Sixth Circuit Court of Appeals let the program stay in place pending all appeals.

Around the same time, Congress debated a bill to allow warrantless surveillance.[24] In 2007, Attorney General Alberto Gonzales announced that the warrantless NSA program would end. The government would submit all future surveillance requests to the FISA court, as the law required.[25]

Less than seven months later, however, Congress amended FISA to allow warrantless surveillance. Although the law would expire in six months, critics felt outraged.[26] Despite all the public outcry, it seemed as if Congress was giving the executive branch free rein for spying.

Before then, about half the people surveyed in a *USA Today*/Gallup poll had said President Bush's administration had gone "too far" in expanding presidential power.[27] Yet there were some signs that Congress might yet push back.

Liberal Democrats such as Senators Feingold and Patrick Leahy (D-Vt.) have argued that the executive branch should not abuse or exceed its powers. Moderate politicians have been critical too, including Ron Wyden (D-Oreg.), Chuck Grassley (R-Iowa), and Arlen Specter (R-Pa.).[28] By voicing criticisms, they helped shape legislation.

Of course, the ultimate check on political power is how

people vote. During the 2006 election campaigns, hot topics included dissatisfaction with the economy and the war in Iraq. Control of both the Senate and House of Representatives swung to the Democratic Party.

When different political parties control Congress and the executive branch, the president has a harder time getting laws passed. Congress may look closer at executive actions too.

In 2007, the new Congress began working on new laws. Some bills would repeal prior laws. Others would restrict agency actions. Still others might approve or expand them.

Such review will not necessarily change the reach of executive power. Ideally, however, it should help keep it in check. Otherwise, there is always the next round of elections.

Know Your Rights

Civil rights groups continue to be the most vocal critics of homeland security programs. The media plays a big role too, by reporting on agency activities.

The government says that only guilty parties should fear its efforts. Yet civil rights groups say thousands of innocent Americans have been caught up in the government's surveillance net.

At best, civil rights groups argue, the government's actions invade citizens' privacy. At worst, they might trigger a new era of McCarthyism. After all, the government says it is only pursuing potential terrorists. But what is to keep it from going after political enemies too?

Just as the government may stay silent about many of its victories in preventing terrorist attacks, it is also likely to keep quiet about the full extent of its surveillance work. Thus, the programs the public knows about may be just the tip of the iceberg.

Throughout history, America has faced threats to its security. At times, the government has limited individuals' freedoms.

Each time, its supporters argued that such steps were necessary to protect the country. And the government usually lifted any restrictions after the threat passed. Supporters of the government's homeland security program say any small inconveniences are worth the price of protecting America.

Yet it is unclear when the threat of terrorism will end, if ever. Champions of civil liberties argue that the government should not overstep its powers and infringe on individual freedoms even a little.

As Benjamin Franklin once wrote: "They that can give up essential liberty to obtain a little temporary safety deserve

Becoming informed about what to do in emergencies is one way of dealing with threats. Knowing your rights as well as your responsibilities in a democracy is also crucial.

neither liberty nor safety."[29] In other words, the quest for safety is no excuse to trample on individual rights.

At a minimum, the debate highlights the need for America's citizens to learn about developments and to know their rights. The September 11 attacks showed that twenty-first century America cannot take its safety for granted.

At the same time, Americans cannot take their freedoms and rights for granted, either. All citizens have a duty to know their rights and to protect them. As antislavery advocate Wendell Phillips and others have argued, "Eternal vigilance is the price of liberty."[30]

Keep current on developments in the war on terrorism. Use news sources in print, on the air, and online. At the same time, watch out for possible abuses of your own civil rights or those of others.

Consider the pros and cons of homeland security programs. Find out where political candidates stand on different issues. You could even hold a debate in your class or with friends when news stories break.

The homeland security program's ultimate goal is to protect Americans and their freedoms. Everyone has a huge stake in that.

Chapter Notes

Chapter 1. Terror Strikes in America

1. "9/11 by the Numbers," *New York Magazine*, 2006, <http://www.newyorkmetro.com/news/articles/wtc/1year/numbers.htm> (August 24, 2006).

2. Jerry Adler, "Connecting in New York," *Newsweek*, September 27, 2001, p. 24.

3. Karen Breslau, "Courage in the Air," *Newsweek*, September 27, 2001, p. 32.

4. *The 9/11 Commission Report: Final Report of the National Commission on Terrorist Attacks upon the United States* (New York: W.W. Norton & Co., 2004), pp. 10–14; Breslau; "What Happened on Tuesday, September 11, 2001: A Timeline of Terror," *National Geographic*, n.d., <http://channel.national geographic.com/channel/inside911/timeline.html> (August 1, 2006).

5. "Remarks by President Bush from Barksdale Air Force Base," September 11, 2001, <http://www.americanrhetoric.com/speeches/gwbush911barksdale.htm> (August 1, 2006).

6. Michael Hirsch et al., "We've Hit The Targets," *Newsweek*, September 13, 2001, p. 36.

7. 28 C.F.R. §0.85.

8. 22 U.S.C. §2656f(d); see also "Patterns of Global Terrorism, 2000," Department of State, April 30, 2001, <http://www.state.gov/s/ct/rls/pgtrpt/2000/index.cfm?docid=2419> (March 26, 2007).

9. "DOD Dictionary of Military and Associated Terms," Department of Defense, August 8, 2006, <http://www.dtic.mil/doctrine/jel/doddict/data/t/05436.html> (March 26, 2007).

10. Federal Bureau of Investigation memorandum, July 10, 2001 (redacted and unclassified), <http://www.usdoj.gov/oig/special/0506/app2.htm> (August 7, 2006); "A Review of the FBI's Handling of Intelligence Information Prior to the September 11

Attacks," Chapter 3, November 2004, <http://www.usdoj.gov/oig/special/0506/chapter3.htm#II> (August 7, 2006).

11. *The 9/11 Commission Report*, p. xv; Public Law 107-306, 116 Stat. 2383, November 27, 2002.

12. "Address to a Joint Session of Congress and the American People," Office of the White House, September 20, 2001, <http://www.whitehouse.gov/newsreleases/2001/09/20010920-8.html> (August 2, 2006).

13. Brian Knowlton, "Many Vacancies at Homeland Security," *New York Times*, July 9, 2007, <http://www.nytimes.com/2007/07/09/washington/09cnd-secure.html?ex=1188446400&en=1bc7be36e5ec2fc7&ei=5070> (August 28, 2007).

14. Mimi Hall, "Ex-Official Tells of Homeland Security Failures," *USA Today*, December 28, 2004, p. 7A.

Chapter 2. **Security and America's History**

1. "An Act in Addition to the Act Entitled 'An Act for the Punishment of Crimes Against the United States,'" July 14, 1798, posted by the Avalon Project at Yale Law School, 1997, <http://www.yale.edu/lawweb/avalon/statutes/sedact.htm> (August 3, 2006); "An Act Respecting Alien Enemies," July 6, 1798, posted by the Avalon Project at Yale Law School, 1997, <http://www.yale.edu/lawweb/avalon/statutes/alien.htm> (August 3, 2006).

2. *Ex parte Merryman*, 17 F.Cas. 144 (1861).

3. *Ex parte Milligan*, 71 U.S. 2, 122, 126 (1866).

4. *Schenck* v. *United States*, 249 U.S. 47, 52 (1919). See generally William H. Rehnquist, *All the Laws But One: Civil Liberties in Wartime* (New York: Vintage Books, 2000), pp. 171–183.

5. Wallace Carroll, "Japanese Spies Showed the Way for Raid on Vital Areas in Hawaii," *New York Times*, December 31, 1941, p. 3; Charles Hurd, "Heroic Acts Cited," *New York Times*, December 16, 1941, p. 1.

6. Executive Order 9066, 7 Fed. Reg. 1407 (February 19, 1942), <http://historymatters.gmu.edu/d/5154> (July 31, 2006).

7. *Korematsu* v. *United States*, 323 U.S. 214, 218 (1944).

8. *Korematsu* v. *United States*, 323 U.S. 214, 233 (1944) (Murphy, J., dissenting).

9. Civil Liberties Act of 1988, Public Law 100-383, 102 Stat. 903 (1988).

10. *Adler* v. *Board of Education*, 385 U.S. 485, 510 (Douglas, J., dissenting).

11. Paul Malone, "Clinton Regrets Missed Chance," *Daily Telegraph* (Sydney, Australia), September 20, 2001, World, p. 4; Bill Hutchinson, "U.S. Thwarted Four Bin Laden Attacks, Clinton Says," *New York Daily News*, September 19, 2001, News, p. 24.

Chapter 3. **Don't Sacrifice Civil Liberties!**

1. Mohamad Bazzi, "Storm over CIA, His Case," *Newsday*, March 11, 2007, p. A30.

2. Adam Liptak, "U.S. Appeals Court Upholds Dismissal of Abuse Suit Against C.I.A., Saying Secrets Are at Risk," *New York Times*, March 3, 2007, p. A6.

3. Katherine Shrader, "Rockefeller: Should CIA Prisons Stay?" *Washington Post online*, March 24, 2007, <http://www.washingtonpost.com/wpdyn/content/article/2007/03/24/AR20070 32400449.html?sub=AR> (March 28, 2007).

4. Michael Fletcher, "Bush Signs Terrorism Measure," *Washington Post*, October 18, 2006, p. A4.

5. "President Bush Signs Un-American Military Commissions Act," American Civil Liberties Union, October 17, 2006, <http://www.aclu.org/safefree/detention/27091prs20061017.html> (October 17, 2006); see also Nat Hentoff, "Detainees Compromise: Lose-lose," *USA Today*, September 27, 2006, p. 13A.

6. *Boumediene* v. *Bush*, 75 U.S.L.W. 3528 (April 2, 2007); see also "Guantanamo Follies," *New York Times*, April 6, 2007, p. A18; Warren Richey, "Little Redress in US Courts for Detainees," *Christian Science Monitor*, April 3, 2007, p. 1; David L. McColgin,

"Guantanamo: Five Years and Counting," *Pittsburgh Post-Gazette*, March 4, 2007, p. H1.

7. 153 Cong. Rec. S.1918 (February 13, 2007).

8. "Department of Justice Inspector General Issues Report on Treatment of Aliens Held on Immigration Charges in Connection with the Investigation of the September 11 Terrorist Attacks," United States Department of Justice, Office of the Inspector General, June 2, 2003, pp. 1–5, <http://www.usdoj.gov/oig/special/0306/press.pdf> (September 29, 2006). See generally "The September 11 Detainees: A Review of the Treatment of Aliens Held on Immigration Charges in Connection with the Investigation of the September 11 Attacks," United States Department of Justice, Office of the Inspector General, April 2003, <http://www.usdoj.gov/oig/special/0306/full.pdf> (September 29, 2006).

9. *Turkmen* v. *Ashcroft*, Case No. 02 CV 2307 (JG), 2006 U.S. Dist. LEXIS 39170 (E.D.N.Y., June 14, 2006); see also Nina Bernstein, "Echoes of '40's Internment Are Seen in Muslim Detainees Suit," *New York Times*, April 3, 2007, p. B1.

10. James J. Zogby, "Statement before the United States Senate Committee on the Judiciary," November 18, 2003, <http://www.globalsecurity.org/security/library/congress/2003_h/031118-zogby.htm> (September 29, 2006). See also "Homeland Security: Justice Department's Project to Interview Aliens after September 11, 2001," General Accounting Office, April 2003, pp. 5, 13–17, <http://www.gao.gov/new.items/d03459.pdf> (September 29, 2006); Peter Grier, "Fragile Freedoms," *Christian Science Monitor*, December 13, 2001, p. 1.

11. Jim Kouri, ""The ACLU and Airport Security," *The National Ledger*, August 16, 2006, <http://www.nationalledger.com/artman/publish/article_27267740.shtml> (August 24, 2006).

12. James Risen and Eric Lichtblau, with Barclay Walsh, "Bush Lets U.S. Spy on Callers Without Courts," *New York Times*, December 16, 2005, p. A1.

13. Leslie Cauley, "NSA Has Massive Database of Americans' Phone

Calls," *USA Today*, May 11, 2006, p. 1A; Leslie Cauley, "Data Cover Billions of Phone Calls," *USA Today*, May 11, 2006, p. 5A; see also John Diamond and David Jackson, "Furor Erupts Over NSA's Secret Phone Call Database," *USA Today*, May 12, 2006, p. 1A.

14. "NSA Has Your Phone Records," *USA Today*, May 12, 2006, p. 14A.

15. "Daily Show Celebrity Interview—Howard Dean," May 15, 2006, <http://www.comedycentral.com/sitewide/media_player/play.jhtml ?itemId=69103> (October 11, 2006).

16. Joe Swartz and Kevin Johnson, "U.S. Asks Internet Firms to Save Data," *USA Today*, June 1, 2006, p. 1A; see also "One-click Snooping," *Los Angeles Times*, June 5, 2006, p. B10; Saul Hansell and Eric Lichtblau, "U.S. Wants Internet Companies to Keep Web-Surfing Records," *New York Times*, June 2, 2006, p. A15.

17. Arshad Mohammed and Sara Kehaulani Goo, "Government Increasingly Turning to Data Mining," *Washington Post*, June 15, 2006, p. D3.

18. Warren Mass, "The NSA and Domestic Spying," *New American*, July 24, 2006, p. 25.

19. Patrick Leahy, "Is the National Security Agency's Domestic Surveillance Program Legal?" *Congressional Digest*, April 2006, pp. 107, 109.

20. *A Review of the Federal Bureau of Investigation's Use of National Security Letters*, U.S. Department of Justice, Office of Inspector General, March, 2007, pp. 122–123, <http://www.usdoj.gov/oig/special/s0703b/final.pdf> (March 9, 2007).

21. R. Jeffrey Smith, "FBI Violations May Number 3,000, Official Says," *Washington Post*, March 21, 2007, p. A7.

22. R. Jeffrey Smith, "Report Details Missteps in Data Collection," *Washington Post*, March 10, 2007, p. A1.

23. Leahy.

24. "Daily Show Celebrity Interview—Howard Dean."

25. "National Security Whistleblowers," American Civil Liberties Union, 2005, <http://www.aclu.org/safefree/general/

18830prs20050804.html> (October 23, 2006); see also David Rose, "An Inconvenient Patriot," *Vanity Fair*, September 2005, pp. 264–282.

26. Richard Willing, "With Only a Letter, FBI Can Gather Private Data," *USA Today*, July 6, 2006, p. 1A; Dan Eggen, "FBI Sought Data on Thousands in '05," *Washington Post*, May 2, 2006, p. A4.

27. June Sandra Neal, "A Patriotic Act: How Four Connecticut Librarians Faced Down the Government to Protect Their Patrons' Constitutional Rights," *Hartford Courant*, September 24, 2006, NE Magazine, p. 4.

28. Eric Lichtblau, James Risen, and Barclay Walsh, "Bank Data Sifted in Secret by U.S. to Block Terror," *New York Times*, June 23, 2006, p. A1.

29. Ibid.

30. Peter Baker, "Surveillance Disclosure Denounced; 'Disgraceful,' Says Bush of Reports," *Washington Post*, June 27, 2006, p. A1.

31. Sheryl Gay Stolberg and Eric Lichtblau, "Cheney Assails Press on Report on Bank Data," *New York Times*, June 24, 2006, p. A1.

32. Faye Fiore, "Congressman Wants N.Y. Times Prosecuted," *Los Angeles Times*, June 26, 2006, p. A5.

33. "Patriotism and the Press," *New York Times*, June 28, 2006, p. A20.

34. Fiore.

Chapter 4. Saving America from Grave Threats

1. Peter Grief, "Fragile Freedoms," *Christian Science Monitor*, December 13, 2001, p. 1.

2. Alberto Gonzales, "Is the National Security Agency Domestic Surveillance Program Legal?" *Congressional Digest*, April 2006, p. 106.

3. Ronald Kessler, "Wiretap Dance," *Wall Street Journal*, December 21, 2005, p. A18.

4. David E. Sanger and Eric Schmitt, "Cheney's Power No Longer

Goes Unquestioned," *New York Times,* September 10, 2006, sec. 1, p. 1; Richard Stevenson and Adam Liptak, "Cheney Defends Eavesdropping Without Warrants," *New York Times,* December 21, 2005, p. A36.

5. "President's Radio Address," Office of the White House, December 17, 2005, <http://www.whitehouse.gov/news/releases/2005/12/20051217.html> (October 5, 2006); see also Chitra Ragavan, "The Letter of the Law," *U.S. News & World Report,* March 27, 2006, p. 27.

6. Neil King, Jr., "Wiretap Furor Widens Republican Divide," *Wall Street Journal,* December 22, 2005, p. A4.

7. Mike DeWine, e-mail correspondence to author, July 26, 2006.

8. "Authorization for Use of Military Force," 107th Congress, 1st Sess., S.J. Res. 23 (September 14, 2001).

9. "Administration Position: Justification for Warrantless Wiretapping," *Congressional Digest,* April 2006, p. 98.

10. Victoria Toensing, "Constitutional Surveillance," *Weekly Standard,* March 6, 2006, (through InfoTrac OneFile, October 5, 2006); *Hamdi* v. *Rumsfeld,* 542 U.S. 507 (2004).

11. Mortimer Zuckerman, "Using All the Tools," *U.S. News & World Report,* February 27, 2006, p. 80.

12. *The 9/11 Commission Report: Final Report of the National Commission on Terrorist Attacks upon the United States* (New York: W.W. Norton & Co., 2004), p. 382.

13. "Remarks by the Secretary of Homeland Security Michael Chertoff at the International Association of Chiefs of Police Annual Conference," October 16, 2006, <http://www.dhs.gov/xnews/speeches/sp_1161184338115.shtm> (October 30, 2006).

14. "President Bush Discusses NSA Surveillance Program," Office of the White House, May 11, 2006, <http://www.whitehouse.gov/news/releases/2006/05/20060511-1.html> (October 5, 2006); see also Mark Hosenball and Evan Thomas, "Hold the Phone: Big Brother Knows Whom You Call," *Newsweek,* May 22, 2006, p. 22.

15. Jay Winik, "Security Comes Before Liberty," *Wall Street Journal,* October 23, 2001, p. A26.

16. Michael Chertoff, Testimony before the House Homeland Security Committee, April 13, 2005, quoted at "Michael Chertoff on Civil Rights," n.d., <http://www.ontheissues.org/Cabinet/Michael_Chertoff_Civil_Rights.htm> (October 30, 2006).

17. Gonzales.

18. Evan Thomas and Michael Hirsh, "The Debate Over Torture," *Newsweek*, November 21, 2005, p. 26.

19. "President Bush Signs Military Commissions Act of 2006," Office of the White House, October 17, 2006, <http://www.whitehouse.gov/news/releases/2006/10/20061017-1.html> (October 17, 2006); Michael A. Fletcher, "Bush Signs Terrorism Measure," *Washington Post*, October 18, 2006, p. A4.

20. Thomas and Hirsh.

21. Rick Klein, "Deal Made on Detainee Questioning," *Boston Globe*, September 22, 2006.

22. "President Bush Signs Military Commissions Act of 2006"; Michael A. Fletcher, "Bush Signs Terrorism Measure," *Washington Post*, October 18, 2006, p. A4.

23. Bill Carter and Felicity Barringer, "Networks Agree to U.S. Request to Edit Future bin Laden Tapes," *New York Times*, October 11, 2006, p. A1.

24. Mark Jurkowitz, "Coverage of War Dead Triggers Fierce Debate," *Boston Globe*, May 4, 2004, p. C15.

25. Eric Lichtblau, Scott Shane, and Ken Belson, "Bush Is Pressed Over New Report on Surveillance," *New York Times*, May 12, 2006, p. A1.

26. Jim VandeHei, "Bush Reasserts Presidential Prerogatives," *Washington Post*, January 27, 2006, p. A6.

27. "Following Rumsfeld, Supporters Asserted That Criticism of Defense Secretary Helps America's Enemies," Media Matters for America, April 20, 2006, <http://mediamatters.org/items/200604200008> (April 3, 2007).

28. "Robertson Called Democratic War Criticism 'Treason,'" Media Matters for America, December 12, 2005, <http://mediamatters.org/items/200512120002> (October 19, 2006).

29. David Jackson, "Bush, Kerry Snipe as Campaign Gets Nastier," *USA Today*, November 1, 2006, p. 6A; Adam Nagourney and Jim Rutenberg, "As Vote Nears, Stances on War Set Off Sparks," *New York Times*, November 1, 2006, p. A1.

30. Rosa Ehrenreich Brooks, "War Everywhere: Rights, National Security Law, and the Law of Armed Conflict in the Age of Terror," *University of Pennsylvania Law Review*, December 2004, pp. 675, 676, n. 5; Jonathan Turley, "Art and the Constitution: The Supreme Court and the Rise of the Impressionist School of Constitutional Interpretation," *Cato Supreme Court Review*, 2003–2004, pp. 69, 104, n. 135.

31. Shira A. Scheindlin and Matthew L. Schwartz, "With All Due Deference: Judicial Responsibility in a Time of Crisis," *Hofstra Law Review*, Spring 2004, pp. 795, 801 & n. 25; John Lichtenthal, "Note: The Patriot Act and Bush's Military Tribunals: Effective Enforcement or Attacks on Civil Liberties?" *Buffalo Human Rights Law Review*, 2004, pp. 399, 426; William H. Rehnquist, *All the Laws But One: Civil Liberties in Wartime* (New York: Vintage Books, 2000), p. 223.

32. Lee Epstein, et al., "The Supreme Court During Crisis: How War Affects Only Non-war Cases," *New York University Law Review*, April 2005, pp. 1, 3 & n. 6.

33. "President Discusses Global War on Terror," Office of the White House, September 29, 2006, <http://www.whitehouse.gov/news/releases/2006/09/20060929-3.html> (October 2, 2006).

34. *Trends 2005*, Pew Research Center, 2005, p. 4, <http://pewresearch.org/assets/files/trends2005.pdf> (October 2, 2006).

35. Andrew Bacevich, "The Cult of National Security: What Happened to Checks and Balances?" *Commonweal*, January 27, 2006, p. 7.

Chapter 5. **Protection in Practice**

1. "Federal Funding for Homeland Security," Congressional Budget Office, April 30, 2004, <http://www.cbo.gov/showdoc.cfm?index=5414&sequence=0> (October 6, 2006).

2. "Progress in Developing the National Asset Database," Department of Homeland Security, Office of the Inspector General, June 2006, pp. 5, 12–13, <http://www.dhs.gov/interweb/assetlibrary/OIG_06-40_Jun06.pdf> (October 7, 2006).

3. "War on Terre Haute," *The Daily Show*, August 10, 2006; see also Spencer Hsu, "U.S. Struggles to Rank Potential Terror Targets," *Washington Post*, July 16, 2006, p. A9, <http://www.comedycentral.com/motherload/index.jhtml?ml_video=72795> (September 14, 2006); and Eric Lipton, "Come One, Come All, Join the Terror Target List," *New York Times*, July 12, 2006, p. A1.

4. "War on Terre Haute."

5. "Fact Sheet: An Overview of America's Security Since 9/11," Department of Homeland Security, 2005, <http://www.dhs.gov/dhspublic/interapp/press_release/press_release_0505.xml> (June 1, 2006).

6. Becky Akers, "A Better Way Than the TSA," *Christian Science Monitor*, March 21, 2007, p. 9; Lisa Mysers and Rich Gardella, "Airline Screeners Fail Government Bomb Tests," MSNBC, March 17, 2006, <http://www.msnbc.msn.com/id/11863165> (April 18, 2007).

7. Ron Marsico, "Airport Screeners Fail to See Most Test Bombs," *Seattle Times*, October 28, 2006, p. A5.

8. Mark K. Matthews and Beth Kassab, "Smuggle Case Shows a Security Gap at Airports," *Los Angeles Times*, March 11, 2007, p. A30; Associated Press, "Boy, 9, Sneaks onto Jetliner in Seattle, Makes It to Texas," *Houston Chronicle*, January 18, 2007, p. B4.

9. "Once Again, TSA Shrinks from Responsibility to Scan Cargo Placed on Passenger Planes," Office of Edward Markey, May 17, 2006, <http://markey.house.gov/index.php?option=com_content&task=view&id=1587&Itemid=72> (September 28, 2006); see also Kimberly Atkins and Casey Ross, "9/11 Five Years Later: Markey Rips Bush over Safety Policies," *Boston Herald*, September 9, 2006, News, p. 5; Andy Pasztor, "Freighted with Worry," *Wall Street Journal*, August 15, 2006, p. B1.

10. "ACLU Sues U.S. over 'No-Fly' List," *CNN.com*, April 6, 2004, <http://www.cnn.com/2004/LAW/04/06/no.fly.lawsuit> (July 23, 2006).

11. Gina Davis, "What's In a Name? For Some, a Hassle," *Baltimore Sun*, June 11, 2006, p. 1A.

12. Jeffrey Passel, "Size and Characteristics of the Unauthorized Migrant Population in the United States," Pew Hispanic Center, March 7, 2006, <http://pewhispanic.org/reports/report.php? ReportID=61> (October 6, 2006).

13. "SBInet: Securing U.S. Borders," U.S. Customs and Border Protection, September 2006, <http://www.cbp.gov/linkhandler/ cgov/newsroom/fact_sheets/border/secure_border_initiative/sbinet _factsheet.ctt/sbinet_factsheet.pdf> (October 6, 2006).

14. "President Bush Signs Department of Homeland Security Appropriations Act," Office of the White House, October 4, 2006, <http://www.whitehouse.gov/news/releases/2006/10/20061004- 2.html> (October 6, 2006).

15. Jacques Billeaud, "Border Patrol Hiring Push Raises Worry about Standards," *Cincinnati Enquirer*, April 22, 2007, p. A5.

16. Geoff Brumfiel and Heidi Ledford, "Safe Passage," *Nature*, September 7, 2006, pp. 6–7.

17. "Feds Don't Appeal Ramadan Decision," *South Bend Tribune*, August 26, 2006, p. B1; "Judge Sets Ramadan Deadline," *South Bend Tribune*, August 26, 2006, p. B1; Margaret Fosmoe, "Muslim Scholar Resigns Notre Dame Position," *South Bend Tribune*, December 15, 2004, p. A1.

18. Waskar Ari, e-mail communication to author, August 23, 2007; Melissa Lee, "Bolivian Professor Coming to UNL," *Lincoln Journal Star*, July 20, 2007, p. A1.

19. Beth Givens, "Alert: Real ID Act Will Increase Exposure to ID Theft," February 28, 2007, <http://www.privacyrights.org/ar/ real_id_act.htm> (April 21, 2007); American Civil Liberties Union, "Real Nightmare: About the Issue," n.d., <http://www.realnightmare.org/about/21> (April 21, 2007).

20. "Washington Governor Signs Bill Rejecting Real ID," April 18,

2007, <http://www.aclu.org/privacy/gen/29426prs20070418.html> (April 21, 2007); "The Real(ID) World," *Omaha World Herald,* October 18, 2006, p. 6B. See also S. 717, 110th Congo, 1st Sesso. (bill to amend REAL ID Act of 2005).

21. Andrea Elliott, "5 Muslims to Sue Homeland Security in Border Detentions," *New York Times,* April 20, 2005, p. B3.

22. "Preparing Makes Sense. Get Ready Now," Department of Homeland Security, 2004, p. 1, <http://www.ready.gov/america/_downloads/Ready_Brochure_Screen_EN_20040129.pdf> (October 4, 2006).

23. Ibid.; Macon Morehouse, "Man with a Plan," *People Weekly,* March 17, 2003, p. 69.

24. Phil Gusman, "Katrina: Devastation on the Gulf Coast," *Claims,* October 2005, p. 24; Mark E. Ruqet, "Hurricane Rita Adds Billions to Loss Totals," *National Underwriter Property & Casualty-Risk & Benefits Management,* October 3, 2005, p. 6; Daniel Hays and Caroline McDonald, "Downgrades Loom as Katrina Loss Grows," *National Underwriter Property & Casualty-Risk & Benefits Management,* September 19, 2005, p. 6.

25. "President Arrives in Alabama, Briefed on Hurricane Katrina," Office of the White House, press release, September 2, 2005, <http://www.whitehouse.gov/news/releases/2005/09/20050902-2.html> (July 31, 2006).

26. "The Big Disconnect on New Orleans," *CNN.com,* September 2, 2005, <http://www.cnn.com/2005/US/09/02/katrina.response/index.html> (September 14, 2005).

27. Spencer S. Hsu and Susan B. Glasser, "FEMA Director Singled Out by Response Critics," *Washington Post,* September 6, 2005, p. A1.

28. William D. Hartung, "Katrina and the Politics of Security," September 13, 2005, <http://worldpolicy.org/projects/arms/updates/091305Katrina.html> (July 31, 2006).

29. Robert Block, "FEMA Revamp Snubs Homeland Security Chief," *Wall Street Journal,* September 19, 2006, p. A8.

30. "Slow Response," *New Republic,* February 27, 2006, p. 7; see also

Clark Kent Ervin, *Open Target: Where America Is Vulnerable to Attack* (New York: Macmillan, 2006), pp. 180–181.

Chapter 6. Where Do We Go From Here?

1. James Bovard, "The 'Terrorist' Batting Average," *Boston Globe*, July 21, 2006, p. A17.

2. Pamela Ferdinand, "Would-Be Shoe Bomber Gets Life Term," *Washington Post*, January 21, 2003, p. A1; "I Am an Enemy of Your Country; Shoe Bomber Pleads Guilty," *Washington Post*, October 5, 2002, p. A1.

3. Spencer S. Hsu and Robin Wright, "Plot to Attack Transit Tunnels Is Foiled, FBI Says," *Washington Post*, July 9, 2006, p. A13.

4. Walter Pincus, "FBI Role in Terror Probe Questioned; Lawyers Point to Fine Line Between Sting and Entrapment," *Washington Post*, September 2, 2006, p. A1.

5. Dan Eggen, "Georgia Pair Charged in Plot to Strike Capitol, World Bank," *Washington Post*, July 20, 2006, p. A12.

6. Amy Fagan and Charles Hurt, "Democrats Say U.S. Less Safe Since 9/11," *Washington Times* online, September 6, 2006, <http://www.washingtontimes.com/functions/print.php?StoryID= 20060906-122514-3148r> (September 11, 2006).

7. Amy Westfeldt, "Ground Zero Falls Silent to Mark 9/11," *Yahoo! News*, September 11, 2006, <http://news.yahoo.com/s/ap/ 20060911/ap_on_re_us/sept11_rdp> (September 11, 2006).

8. "Remarks by Secretary of Homeland Security Michael Chertoff on September 11: Five Years Later," September 8, 2006, <http://www.dhs.gov/dhspublic/interapp/speech/speech_0287.xml> (September 11, 2006).

9. John Mueller, "Is There Still a Terrorist Threat? The Myth of the Omnipresent Enemy," *Foreign Affairs*, September/October 2006, pp. 2–8; see also Jesse Walker and Nick Gillespie, "The State of War and Domestic Terrorism: Where We're At, Five Years After the 9/11 Attacks," *Reason*, October 2006, p. 28.

10. Nathan Burchfiel, "Biden Says America Not Safer, Al-Qaeda Planning Attacks," *CNSnews.com*, September 8, 2006,

<http://www.cnsnews.com/ViewNation.asp?Page=/Nation/archive/200609/NAT20060908b.html> (September 11, 2006).

11. Bruce Riedel, "Al Qaeda Strikes Back," *Foreign Affairs*, May/June 2007, p. 24.

12. Zöe Baird, James Barksdale, et al., *Creating a Trusted Network for Homeland Security*, Markle Foundation, 2003, p. 14, <http://www.markle.org/downloadable_assets/nstf_report2_full_report.pdf> (October 17, 2006).

13. Michael Crowley, "Playing Defense," *The New Republic*, March 15, 2004, pp. 17, 19.

14. Ibid., p. 17.

15. Evan F. Kohlmann, "The Real Online Terrorist Threat," *Foreign Affairs*, September/October 2006, pp. 115–124.

16. Dan Eggen, "FBI Agents Still Lacking Arabic Skills," *Washington Post*, October 11, 2006, p. A1.

17. Mimi Hall, "Ex-Official Tells of Homeland Security Failures," *USA Today*, December 28, 2004, p. 7A.

18. James Taranto, "The Weekend Interview with Dick Cheney: A Strong Executive," *Wall Street Journal*, January 28, 2006, p. A8.

19. Russ Feingold, "Is the National Security Agency's Domestic Surveillance Program Legal?" *Congressional Digest*, April 2006, pp. 111, 115, 117.

20. "Congressional Research Service Analysis: Constitutional and Statutory Framework for NSA Activities," *Congressional Digest*, April 2006, pp. 99–102.

21. John W. Dean, "Vice President Cheney and the Fight Over 'Inherent' President Powers: His Attempt to Swing the Pendulum Back Began Long Before 9/11," FindLaw, February 10, 2006, <http://writ.news.findlaw.com/dean/20060210.html> (October 17, 2006).

22. Jeffrey Rosen, "Tap Dance," *New Republic*, February 27, 2006, p. 10; Michael Isikoff, Mark Hosenball, and Evan Thomas, "Bush's Bad Connection," *Newsweek*, February 20, 2006, p. 30.

23. Caroline Frederickson, "Is the National Security Agency's Domestic

Surveillance Program Legal?" *Congressional Digest*, April 2006, pp. 123, 127.

24. Richard Simon and Richard B. Schmitt, "Wiretap, Tribunal Bills Get Senatorial Shuffle," *Los Angeles Times*, September 26, 2006, p. A12.

25. Donna Leinwand, "Court To Oversee Wiretap Program," *USA Today*, January 18, 2007, p. 1A.

26. Eric Mink, "The Relentless President: Congress Caves on Spying," *St. Louis Post-Dispatch*, August 8, 2007, p. C9; Donna Leinwand and David Jackson, "New Law Widens Government's Right to Listen In," *USA Today*, August 6, 2007, p. 7A; Ellen Nakashima and Joby Warrick, "House Approves Wiretap Measure," *Washington Post*, August 5, 2007, p. A1.

27. Susan Page, "Power Play: Congress Pushing Back Against Bush's Expansion of Presidential Authority," *USA Today*, June 6, 2006, p. 1A.

28. Jeffrey Rosen, "Privacy Pleas," *New Republic*, May 16, 2003, pp. 19–21.

29. "Eternal Vigilance Is the Price of Liberty," *freedomkeys.com*, 2004, <http://freedomkeys.com/vigil.htm> (September 11, 2006); Adam Cohen, "Justice Rehnquist's Ominous History of Wartime Freedom," *New York Times*, September 22, 2002, sec. 4, p. 12.

30. "Eternal Vigilance Is the Price of Liberty"; "Respectfully Quoted: A Dictionary of Quotations, 1989," *Bartleby.com*, <http://www.bartleby.com/73/1073.html> (September 11, 2006).

Glossary

al-Qaeda—The terrorist network headed by Osama bin Laden that attacked the World Trade Center and Pentagon on September 11, 2001.

appeal—A higher court's review of a lower court's decision on a legal matter.

constitutional—Consistent with or allowed by the terms of the Constitution; something that goes against the Constitution is unconstitutional.

electronic surveillance—Using electronic equipment to eavesdrop or otherwise get information; examples include tracking or monitoring of telecommunications and/or computer activity and equipment for purposes of gaining information.

executive—Of or relating to the actions of the branch of government charged with carrying out the laws; for the federal government, the executive branch is headed by the President and includes numerous administrative agencies.

ex parte—Technically, without the other side of a dispute present; the term is sometimes used in habeas corpus cases.

habeas corpus—Literally, to have the body; a writ of habeas corpus requires that a prisoner be brought before a judge for review of the lawfulness of that person's imprisonment.

judicial—Of or relating to a court of law.

legislative—Of or having to do with the passage of laws.

network—An organization of associated individuals with a common interest or cause.

ratify—To approve by official action.

rescind—To cancel, revoke, or withdraw.

rhetoric—Persuasive language of the type used in public speeches.

terrorism—The use or threat of unlawful violence to exert power over people through fear, for political, religious, or similar goals.

visa—A government document that grants permission for someone to enter from another country.

warrant—Authorization by a judicial body to let law enforcement personnel take specific actions; for example, a search warrant lets police search a person or property for items described in it.

Further Reading

Beyer, Mark. *Homeland Security and Weapons of Mass Destruction: How Prepared Are We?* New York: Rosen Publishing Group, 2005.

Campbell, Geoffrey A. *A Vulnerable America: An Overview of National Security.* San Diego: Lucent Books, 2003.

Downing, David. *The War on Terrorism: The First Year.* Chicago: Raintree, 2004.

Gottfried, Ted. *Homeland Security versus Constitutional Rights.* Brookfield, Conn.: Twenty-First Century Books, 2003.

Haulley, Fletcher. *The Department of Homeland Security.* New York: Rosen Publishing Group, 2006.

Katz, Samuel M. *U.S. Counterstrike: American Counter-terrorism.* Minneapolis, Minn.: Lerner Publications Company, 2005.

Marguiles, Phillip. *Al Qaeda: Osama bin Laden's Army of Terrorists.* New York: Rosen Publishing Group, 2003.

Marquette, Scott. *America under Attack.* Vero Beach, Fla.: Rourke Publishing, 2003.

Naftali, Timothy. *Blind Spot: The Secret History of American Counterterrorism.* New York: Basic Books, 2005.

Olson, Steven P. *The Homeland Security Act of 2002: Legislation To Protect America.* New York: Rosen Publishing, 2006.

Roleff, Tamara, ed. *America under Attack: Primary Sources.* San Diego: Lucent Books, 2002.

Shostak, Arthur B., ed. *Defeating Terrorism/Developing Dreams: Beyond 9/11 and the Iraq War.* Philadelphia: Chelsea House Publishers, 2004.

Stewart, Gail. *Defending the Borders: The Role of Border and Immigration Control.* San Diego: Lucent Books, 2004.

Torr, James D. *Civil Liberties in the War on Terrorism.* San Diego: Lucent Books, 2004.

Valdez, Angela. *We the People: The U.S. Government's United Response against Terror.* Philadelphia: Chelsea House Publishers, 2002.

Internet Addresses

American Civil Liberties Union
<http://www.aclu.org>

Department of Homeland Security
<http://www.dhs.gov>

Office of Homeland Security
<http://www.whitehouse.gov/homeland>

Index

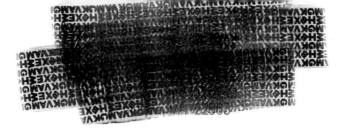

DATE DUE

FOLLETT